MEMORIES OF
THE GREAT & THE GOOD

MEMORIES OF
THE GREAT & THE GOOD

—

ALISTAIR COOKE

PAVILION

This edition published in Great Britain in 1999 by
PAVILION BOOKS LIMITED
London House, Great Eastern Wharf
Parkgate Road, London SW11 4NQ

Published in the United States by
Arcade Publishing, Inc., New York

Designed by API

A CIP catalogue record for this book is available
from the British Library.

ISBN 1 86205 3421

Printed in Great Britain by MPG Books Ltd

4 6 8 10 9 7 5 3

This book can be ordered direct from the publisher.
Please contact the Marketing Department.
But try your bookshop first.

For my son,

John Byrne Cooke

CONTENTS

TO THE READER

The great and the good" is a happy phrase that takes in a general appreciation of some people who are great at one thing and other people whose character is the fascinating thing about them.

The only other point to make about the definition is that a great man or woman is not necessarily a good man or woman. Napoleon was unquestionably a great man and in some conspicuous ways a human monster. There is no need to tease the distinction further for the purpose of this collection, which is to celebrate a variety of well-known people I have met, known, "covered," admired or liked throughout sixty-odd years of journalism. Most of these pieces tend to find, and rejoice in, what is best about their subjects.

Many years ago, I should say shortly after I left Cambridge at the age of twenty-three, I swore off what had been a great fashion among those of us with literary ambitions: the belief, practiced to this day by the intellectual wolf pack of London, New York, and Rome, that the business of literary and historical criticism is the cutting down to size of the famous, of the eminent dead in particular. My temperament was unhappy with the clinical scrutiny of I. A. Richards, then the helmsman of the New Wave in English studies at Cambridge. Too often, it seemed to me, he was determined to discover in a literary work what was phony or meretricious rather than what was admirable. So, I suppose, I can be said to have lapsed into the tradition of Sir Arthur Quiller-Couch's "appreciative" criticism, which Dr. Richards and his pupil William Empson (the first deconstructionist) came along to ridicule and supplant.

There is another prejudice, or post-judice rather, that may have conditioned my choice of heroes and heroines. For many years, my reading has been mainly in biography and in American and British social and political history. And in the past quarter century or so, I have grown increasingly weary of psychobiographies and, even more, of pornobiographies. It is only very rarely (as, for instance, in the biographies of Presidents Cleveland and Clinton) that a person's sex life is crucial to his or her public reputation or performance. Otherwise, erotic probing is simply titillation and pruriency, two words that appear to have vanished from the language of criticism. Even some of the most distinguished biographers today seem plagued by the itch to pry into the sexuality, preferably kinky, of their characters. The plague has passed this book by.

What has made this collection a pleasure to put together is the fact of my having been for all my sixty-odd active years of journalism a foreign correspondent, and for thirty years or more having the privilege of roaming at will around every region of these United States. A foreign correspondent enjoys one or two advantages not given even to distinguished journalists who specialize in one field: labor relations, city hall, the Supreme Court, a sport, and so forth. First is the chance of acquiring what Theodore Roosevelt called "the sense of the continent." And the great reward of the foreign correspondent's trade springs precisely from that freedom to rove around a whole continent. It is the opportunity to meet all sorts and classes of humanity in their native habitat. Had I but life enough and time, I could fill another book with a Dickensian-size cast of memorable unknowns of the greatest variety, whose daily lives I came to look into. Casually now, and at random, I recall soldiers and sailors of every rank, small businessmen of great imagination and comicality, a minor gangster forging U.S. graded beef, a burlesque stripper, a Texas sheep sluicer, a modest, illiterate boy from the Carolinas with a genius for leadership in deadly situations in the Second World War.

Only when I had retired from wandering around America did I make the surprising discovery that the friends of my own friends, and of professional people in general, were invariably people who shared their political prejudices—a drastic method of cutting yourself off from enjoying at least half the human race!

The last two profiles, of Churchill and Bobby Jones, are set apart because I am more certain of them than of the rest (without offense of judgment) that one truly embodied greatness and the other goodness.

Some of these pieces, as the acknowledging note will testify, were originally daily dispatches to my only paper, the (then) *Manchester Guardian*. Five of them are the scripts of radio talks done over the BBC's World Service in my weekly series, "Letters from America." I had written so many thousands of words about President Franklin Roosevelt, from my first White House press conference in 1937 to his funeral at Hyde Park in 1945, that it seemed best to start again and write a new piece focused entirely on one aspect of him, and that the most vividly memorable to me. The same is true of Churchill. When the late William Shawn invited me to have my definitive say about the great man, I employed William Manchester's splendid biography to do so, and that piece, a little expanded, is included here much as it first appeared in *The New Yorker*. The Jones piece was written as the introduction to Martin Davis's recent anthology, *The Greatest of Them All: The Legend of Bobby Jones*.

I cannot end this note without expressing heartfelt gratitude to three people in particular who helped me at a difficult time during the making of this book. First, to my wife Jane, the rocklike, ever-present nurse, companion, best friend; to my publisher, Richard Seaver, for his sainted patience throughout an anxious summer; and, as much as anybody, my secretary, Patricia A. Yasek, whose devotion, tenacity and indestructible cheerfulness under the most trying circumstances made the book publishable in this century.

A.C., Summer 1999

ACKNOWLEDGMENTS

"George Bernard Shaw," "FDR," and "Scotty Reston: The Maestro from Glasgow" were written for this volume.

"John Nance Garner: The Frontiersman," "General Marshall," and "Robert Frost" first aired as radio broadcasts in Alistair Cooke's "Letter from America" series for the BBC and were reprinted in his *Talk About America*, published by Alfred A. Knopf, 1973.

"Frank Lloyd Wright," "Maker of a President: Eleanor Roosevelt," and "The Legend of Gary Cooper" first appeared in the *Manchester Guardian*, and were reprinted in Alistair Cooke's *America Observed*, published by Alfred A. Knopf, 1989.

"Wodehouse at Eighty" first appeared in the *Manchester Guardian*, October 16, 1961, as did "Harold Ross," December 11, 1951; and "Reagan: The Common Man Writ Large," December 29, 1967.

"Dean Acheson" and "The Duke" first appeared in Alistair Cooke's *The Americans*, published by Alfred A. Knopf, 1971.

"Eisenhower at Gettysburg" first appeared in Alistair Cooke's *General Eisenhower on the Military Churchill: A Conversation with Alistair Cooke*, published by W. W. Norton & Co., copyright © 1970 by James Nelson Productions.

"Goldwater: Jefferson in the Desert" first aired as a radio broadcast in Alistair Cooke's "Letter from America" series for the BBC on June 5, 1998; as did "Aiken of Vermont" on November 23, 1984; "Barbara McClintock: The Gene on the Cob" on October 21, 1983; "George Abbott" on February 4, 1995; and "Erma Bombeck: A Rare Bird" on April 26, 1996.

"Chichester: The Master Mariner" first appeared in Alistair Cooke's *Fun & Games,* published in the United Kingdom by Pavilion Books, 1994.

"The Last Victorian" first appeared in *The New Yorker,* August 22, 1983, and was revised for this volume.

"The Gentleman from Georgia" first appeared in Martin Davis's *The Greatest of Them All: The Legend of Bobby Jones,* published by The American Golfer, Inc., 1996, and was revised for this volume.

MEMORIES OF
THE GREAT
&
THE GOOD

1

George Bernard Shaw

(1999)

The Scene: A small conference room in Broadcasting House, the headquarters of the British Broadcasting Corporation, in London.

The Time: The spring of 1935.

The Cast: Sitting around a semicircular formation of long rectangular tables were half a dozen or more very eminent men, assuming postures of confidence and relaxation by which men of equal eminence signify that none of them needs to be impressed by the others. Smoking cigarettes, legs crossed or outstretched, exchanging small talk amiably on one elbow. Modest, not a show-off among them. All, apparently, waiting for the chief or the president, the chairman or whoever.

*   *   *

The roly-poly, merry, bespectacled William Temple, Archbishop of York; Sir Johnston Forbes-Robertson, a regal presence, the last survivor of the Victorian heyday, when an actor was recognizable at a hundred paces; the renowned biologist Julian Huxley, representing Science; Logan Pearsall Smith, a dapper old American expatriate, fashioner of exquisite prose, representing (I suppose) belles lettres, which in the early 1930s was still, in England at any rate, a going profession; and C. K. Ogden, representing—probably—Basic English, for it was unlikely that he had been chosen to serve as the author or explicator of "The Meaning of Meaning," a writhing thesis that nobody cared to have unraveled, not anyway at these meetings. I can't recall now who else was present to represent which of the other arts and sciences. But leaning over a sheaf of papers was a porcine, affable man with clean-shaven jowls. Not, in such company, an equally eminent man but in his own circle, which was that of linguists and phoneticians, a giant: A. Lloyd James, professor of phonetics at the University of London. He was here as the secretary of the board or committee. And what was I, an unknown beginning journalist in his mid-twenties, doing in this assembly of magnificoes? I was just back in England after a two-year stint of graduate work (and play) in the United States. The second year of my American fellowship had been spent at Harvard working under Professor Miles L. Hanley (an American Henry Higgins at the time) on the history of *spoken* English in America, a fascinating field to all, it appeared, but Americans. Registered for this course were three of us, and of the other two one was an Englishwoman. So no assignment could have been more flattering to a novice in a new specialty than an invitation from Professor Lloyd James, who knew about my work, to join this committee as "the referent on American usage."

The committee bore the impressive, and to many people the mysterious, title of: The BBC's Advisory Committee on Spoken English. And before we cue the assembled cast into "action," it is necessary to say something about the founding of this exotic committee, for its title and purpose were popularly misunderstood from its inception. So much so that a useful and civilized institution was killed off within five years and never resurrected.

It had been set up with a single purpose: which was to establish, for the BBC's news and program announcers, a guide to the uniform pronunciation of names, place-names especially, and other words whose educated pronunciation were at the time arousing *cont*roversy (or con*trov*ersy).

What made a large part of the population misunderstand the committee's function was the accent of the announcers. They were a special breed, recruited only after a rigorous test which required them to speak, or at least pronounce, French, German and Italian according to Foreign Office standards. More to the point of the popular complaint, all of them in the London studios were hired because they spoke southern educated English, what was then known to phoneticians and language teachers as Received Standard. "Received by whom?" my headmaster used to intone in a mischievous singsong. With equal monotonous certainty, back came the answer: "The public schools, the Church, the army."

Since the BBC was something quite new to civilization: a radio broadcasting company and then the only one in the nation, it was obvious—if not imperative—that the BBC's spokesmen, the announcers, should not diffuse various forms of educated spoken English. Social democracy had not then invaded England and spread the alien notion that it might be natural for public speech to reflect the variety of regional speech, and that there was no longer any social compulsion to have the educated follow the upper-crust dialect that had evolved from the establishment in the mid-nineteenth century of that most peculiar institution, the English public (i.e. private) school.

But, as I say, the committee was concerned only with setting a uniform standard of pronunciation—of nouns mostly, proper and improper. The uniformity of the announcers' accent was taken for granted. However, they were falsely assumed, most conspicuously by the inhabitants of the Midlands and the North, to be "teaching us how to speak." What the vast majority of midlanders and northerners were hearing from the BBC announcers for the first time in their lives was southern educated speech. By an obvious sleight of mind, what they said they were hearing was "BBC English." This confusion was sufficiently widespread to spawn vaudeville jokes, newspaper cartoons and enough ridicule to belittle and wound the advisory committee's reputation. It was killed off by the Second World War, the oncoming invasion of social democracy and the transatlantic doctrine about the health, the naturalness, the inevitable triumph of "multiculturalism" in democratic societies. Today, educated speech in

England is changing so rapidly that such exemplars as John Gielgud or Nigel Hawthorne will soon be as antediluvian as the vaudeville baritones of Edwardian England. The BBC no longer demands either a uniform accent or pronunciation (except of foreign place-names) and allows its reporters to speak whatever compound or atonal mix of their native woodnotes wild comes naturally to them. So what we are flashing back to is, it only now occurs to me, very much a period piece.

Into this leisurely group—human representatives of the church, literature, the stage, science, belles lettres (no army so far as I can recall), there suddenly intruded an exotic figure indeed, not conceivably a product of the English public school system—a tall, upright, snapdragon old man in an old-fashioned four-button Norfolk tweed suit. He had a glittering eye, and he uttered a peremptory, musically inflected "Gentlemen, let us begin!" It was the chairman himself, George Bernard Shaw. A true British touch was added to this most English institution (not unlike the April-born queen celebrating her birthday in June) by the fact that Shaw himself, who as chairman—and in a tie vote, the supreme arbiter on correct pronunciation—spoke with an unmistakable Dublin brogue and maintained, in the teeth of legions of dissenters, that Dublin was the only place on earth where one could hear "pure spoken English," whatever that was. (This contention occasionally came up in our discussions of pronunciations, but since it was pointed out, usually by Prof. James, that we were confusing specific or particular pronunciations with questions of accent, the chairman would shrug his shoulders, make some final derisory comment in rich Dublinese and pass on.)

The meetings were never less than lively, a spirit practically guaranteed by Shaw's presence and his impish irascibility. (It strikes me, in my own senescence, that perhaps irascibility is a natural reflex of old age: Shaw was, at that first meeting, in his seventy-ninth year.)

A list of the words to be ruled on was handed out to each member, and we first usually disposed of the place-names. They were not chosen arbitrarily for their peculiarity (Buchleuch—*pron.* "Buckloo," Leveson-Gower— *pron.* "Loosen-Gore"), but because they had come up in the news. At one meeting, for instance, we had to pronounce on Marylebone, which had just been the victim of some colorful accident. There was little dispute. It should be noted that most, if not all, of the members were in late middle age, and the old vernacular pronunciation "Marryb'n" was preferred. Shaw accepted the verdict, while noting in a petulant aside that the young, and most people outside London, wouldn't have a notion what the announcer was talking about.

Time and again, the members demonstrated a truth that Hanley had mentioned in the early days as universal: that any group of people, confronted with a word they have known all their lives, and then offered a certain pronunciation, will divide into those who say they've never heard it and those who say they've never heard anything else. This often happened at the committee hearings and when it did, Shaw, rebelling against all his instincts, resorted to the democratic procedure of a vote. When it went against his own preference, he would sigh or incline his head, implying that the winners would rue the day.

The first time I was called on to offer an American alternative was when a clear variation was well-known. In the guide, which the BBC would publish later, the reader would find: "lieutenant—lefftenant (*Am.* loo-tenant)." The committee seemed to accept my function agreeably enough, though Logan Pearsall Smith, as an expatriate Anglophile, hinted from time to time that it would be better if American English did not exist, or at least were never mentioned.

There is a street in London called Conduit Street. The non-Londoners on the committee bowed to the true educated vernacular *Cun-dit*, and the ruling was about to be recorded when Lloyd James, in a spasm of mischief, wondered if Mr. Cooke might like to suggest an alternative American pronunciation. It would not be an exotic word to New Englanders, I said, but plainly an Indian word, cousin to Cotuit, Mass. If so, it would be pronounced Cun-*do*-it. General chuckle and on to business. Only the chairman thought that an American variant should be printed, on the understanding that when the next Irish variation came up, it should get the same treatment. We moved on.

The most memorable little battle happened at a meeting where the simple word "canine" came up for adjudication. Shaw asked each member to pronounce his preference. To a man, they came through: *can*-ine. In spite of the overwhelming preference, Shaw took a vote and, announcing the result, added: "Somebody voted twice." Gentlemanly uproar. I pleaded guilty. "Because, sir," I said, "the American is unquestionably different: it's '*cane*-ine.'" To the disgust of the company, Shaw said firmly: "Quite right!" But, the committee protested, we are unanimous for *can*-ine. Shaw thereupon made a speech, the gist of which was: "I believe strongly in following the pronunciation of men who use the word every day in their profession, and my dentist says, '*cane*-ine.'"

"Then, sir," nipped in the witty Logan Pearsall Smith, "your dentist must be an American."

"Of course!" roared Shaw, "how d'you suppose I came to have all my teeth at my age?"

This retort, I recall, was greeted with a not wholly comprehending chuckle by the assembled Britons, who seemed vaguely unaware of the dim reputation of British dentistry. Shaw beamed on them with a well-satisfied grin, willingly registered the general preference (*can*-ine) but wagged a finger to remind them that he was insisting on "Mr. Cooke's adding in brackets: (*Am. cane*-ine)."

Once the last word had been questioned, argued over and ruled on, the chairman rose to attention, as he had been sitting at attention, and gave an offhand nod, the social equivalent of a thank you and good-bye, stepped down from the rostrum and was out the door. I never remember his mixing with the members or attempting any small talk or socializing in any degree. This was true of the three or four meetings that were held in my time. After a while I could well understand what one or other of the group told me, that Shaw was a man with no friends. In his early, Fabian-campaigning days, he developed at most what you might call enthusiastic acquaintanceships with the other Socialist crusaders, but I can find little evidence, even from his biographer, Hesketh Pearson, that he kept or ever achieved any close friendships at all. Indeed, the notion of Shaw as "a man's man," a normal male with several cronies, is as bizarre as imagining his taking up golf or draw poker.

At one time, in late middle age—say well into his sixties—he socialized, always alone, to the extent of lunching with almost any celebrity who invited him. If they expected a cordial private exchange with a famous public character, they were uniformly disillusioned. The impressions of him from single encounters are strikingly similar. The benevolent P. G. Wodehouse, who liked everybody, was offended by Shaw's coming as a guest to lunch, imagining his host's lavish way of life and deploring it. At another luncheon party, Shaw dismayed the company by teasing H. G. Wells with a joke about his (Wells's) wife's newly diagnosed cancer. At a luncheon in honor of Bergson, Shaw told the guest, simmering with bottled rage, that his philosophy was not what he thought it was. Arriving as a guest of Thomas Masaryk, the founding president of Czechoslovakia, Shaw described the foreign policy of the new country as a disaster and marched from the room. Winston Churchill was unusually laconic: "He was one of my earliest antipathies." James Agate, in the 1930s and 1940s England's most eminent dramatic critic, although he had made it plain in print that "Shaw's plays are the price we have to pay for his prefaces," yet thought Shaw to be the greatest living polemical writer and "a very great man." Agate was delirious when Shaw invited him to lunch with Mrs. Shaw and was prepared to sit and worship: "He sat upright in a chair which was frail, spindly and altogether beautiful like himself." Not only did Shaw talk continuously throughout the meal but Agate noticed "an odd habit" (which is surely disturbing to most listeners) "of not looking at you but gazing fixedly at a point somewhere over your shoulder."

When Shaw was the host, however, there is ample record that he could be droll and charming, once it was understood that the available food was to be the vegetarian platter prepared by Mrs. Shaw and that the guests had been invited to be present at a monologue. "Although," Bertrand Russell recalled, "like many witty men he considered wit an adequate substitute for wisdom, he could defend any idea, however silly, so cleverly as to make those who did not accept it look like fools."

The meetings of this committee provided my only contact with the great man. It was transitory but vivid and, I now realize, disappointing to a young man who, as an even younger man, had been something of an idolater. At Cambridge I once wrote to him out of the blue and asked him for a photograph and specified, in cocky sophomoric fashion, for "something unusual, not the regular studio portrait." He sent me a sepia photograph of himself lying down on a divan and tossing a bemused smile at the photographer. Underneath, in his beautiful spidery script, he said that this photo was unusual enough to be unique and he hoped it would satisfy me. If it didn't, please to let him know. The tone of the postcard was that of an uncle to a favorite nephew. I was enchanted by it and by the evident cordial good nature of the man himself.

But to most people on the outside who never met him and inferred his private character from his writing, he was a riddle. A young Scottish professor, being invited to lecture on Shaw, replied that she would have to confine her remarks to the plays, for which she had "a great curiosity and respect. As for the man's character, I give up: he is an enigma." What baffled everybody was the inexplicable contradiction between the human being you could meet and see and hear and the public character who was at once a shrewd capitalist, a dedicated Communist, and a defiant admirer of both Hitler and Stalin. This gentle, seemingly reasonable man would certainly hesitate to bruise a gnat but he professed to accept the necessity of liquidating (i.e. murdering) whole regions of peasants for the sake of a long-term political program. Yet the same man could feel excessive guilt for offending a nonentity: a young aspiring writer in the suburbs sent Shaw, evidently for comment, the manuscript of a children's book and its accompanying illustrations. Shaw lost the lot. He subsequently wrote a flock of apologetic letters to the forlorn young man, gave him a part in *The Doctor's Dilemma* and sent him a pair of new boots, a cardigan, an autographed copy of *Man and Superman*, a book on Karl Marx and, for no explained reason, the sum of fifteen pounds, ten shillings.

To the complaint of a London critic that a "wrinkled" Eleanora Duse was appearing in London in a role much too young for her, Shaw retorted: "Her wrinkles are the credentials of her humanity." After unloosing this lance of chivalry and good sense, he was then ready to release a fatuous manifesto proclaiming that vaccination killed more children than it protected.

But the central, and most bewildering, contradiction of his private and public character was that between his personal generosity, courtliness even to the humblest people (his optician remarked to a neighbor—"Oh, that Mr. Shaw! A nice old gentleman, never any trouble at all"), and his lifelong oscillation between maintaining that Stalin's twilight signatures on orders to massacre, torture, exile or "liquidate" were a Tory invention or that they were measures necessary to prevent the Soviet Utopia from sinking into the "debauchery" of democracy.

At the end, I see him leaving Broadcasting House on a late spring morning, a trilby shading his crinkled eyes and white beard, his hands deep in a top coat, marching with his wide tread down Upper Regent Street, occasionally looking over his shoulder for his bus, then deciding the day was balmy enough for walking all the way home. He might pause in one of the leafy London squares to sit on a bench and eat his delicious mid-morning lifesaver of a parsley sandwich. Then on down the Strand to the river and up to his apartment in the Adelphi and reunion with his only friend, wife, companion: the ever-virginal (by mutual agreement in the marriage contract) Charlotte Payne-Townshend. And there, after much meditation, and a lifetime of feeling "the joy in being used for a purpose recognized by yourself as a mighty one," he would sit down and write his will and leave his entire fortune to the mighty purpose of—Simplified Spelling.

2

John Nance Garner:
The Frontiersman
(1967)

On a warm April night in southern Florida, in 1951, two United States senators and a man from Missouri were asleep as holiday guests in the house of a wealthy American statesman, in Hobe Sound, an exclusive strip of land on the ocean, fenced in from the plebs by towering Australian pines and highly cultivated bits of real estate with an asking price of about a hundred thousand dollars* a lot.

Just as the dawn was coming up over the sea and the blue herons that stand motionless in the neighboring lagoons, a telephone startled this silent house and it was answered by the man from Missouri. He was struck dumb by what he heard and he pattered off in his pajamas to the next room and tapped on the door.

* Today—1999—about $1.5 million.

The man from Missouri simply said, "I just had it on the phone from Washington—Harry Truman's fired MacArthur." The senator from Texas came upright, as on a hoist, and sat on the side of the bed and pondered the appalling news: that MacArthur, the hero of the Pacific war, the most Roman of all American generals, had been—as the order said—"stripped of all his commands."

The visible eyeball of the senator from Georgia rolled over the bedsheet and a high southern voice came out from under. "Hitch up yo' pants, Lyndon Johnson," it said, "and let's get the hell back to Washington and get that investigation started or they'll have a posse out for us before noon."

It was a sound instinct. Before the recriminations got started, the three men were back in the capital; and the senator from Georgia began the famous hearings that took many months and, I believe, three million words to affirm the judgment of the president of the United States and to confirm the original prejudices, one way or the other, of its people.

This anecdote is very typical of southern politicians, of their wariness, their healthy respect for the shifts and terrors of public sentiment, their relaxed assumption that pending Judgment Day something practical can be done about almost any catastrophe, from the loss of an election to an earthquake.

It came back to me the other evening when we learned that down on the Mexican border, in Uvalde, Texas, a former vice president of the United States had died. He was John Nance Garner, called "Cactus Jack" after the burning and barren landscape that weaned him. Of all public men today he was the last link between the America of the Civil War and the America of the nuclear age. He would never himself have claimed the title of statesman, and, for that matter, he never earned it. "An elder statesman," he once told Harry Truman, "is a retired politician." He would not have claimed to understand or sympathize with the trouble in the cities, the missions to the moon, or the turn of American life much after 1934. Roosevelt's New Deal was the end of the road for him. And when, at the end of Roosevelt's second term, he stepped down from the vice presidency, he went home to Texas and swore he would never again cross the Potomac River. And he never did. He was cashiered, you might say, by his origins and his prejudices. The Depression overwhelmed him and many more of his breed who had been raised to believe that there was nothing an American couldn't face and overcome if he rolled his sleeves and gritted his teeth and sweated it out.

Today this bluster may sound quite fatuous. But it was a central conviction of the men who tamed the frontier, from the Cumberland Gap to the American River. And John Nance Garner was a fascinating faint echo of it. He was remarkable not for any great gifts of mind or character but for his intense typicality of one aspect of the frontier character: its fatalism, physical hardiness, cynicism, tooth-sucking humor, its humdrum pragmatism in the face of death, disloyalty, and disaster. A Texas judge like Garner demonstrated to perfection the quality once ascribed to W. C. Fields: "He had the greatest reverence for his colleagues, with the usual reservations and suspicions." It is easy to imagine him, a little quiet stoat of a man, hearing the shocked cries of the on-lookers at the severed head of an Indian and glancing down and snapping out, "A flesh wound."

Garner was the son of a Confederate cavalry trooper, and he was born in a muddy cabin, one room wide—what they called in the Red River Valley a shotgun house. Almost all the neighbors lived on farms. The black soil produced cotton and the red clay soil produced corn, and there were little sawmills in the clearings of the shortleaf pine. This was 1868, only three years after the war was over, but not before the Apache raids were over in his part of the country. His horizon was alive with flying squirrels and timber wolves, and his life was bounded by what the farmers called "work-a-crop" parties, by planting and plowing, box-and-pie suppers and fiddlers' contests on Saturday night; and on Sundays by camp meetings, and the whole neighborhood chanting:

> I felt the old shoes on my feet, the glory in my soul,
> The old-time fire upon my lips; the billows ceased to roll.

He was a small chunky man with slant eyes and he was neither pious nor studious. In his *Who's Who* entry, which he kept down to five lines, he put down "limited school advantages," and it was an understatement. But he learned poker from mustered-out soldiers and it stood him in good stead in Washington, where he often in one year won more from his fellow legislators than the ten thousand dollars of his congressional salary. He looked like a cross between a fox and a mole and had many of the more engaging habits of each. He somehow picked up a college education of sorts and at nights he started to read law. This was as practical a calling as any on a frontier which was riddled with army deserters, cattle thieves, claim jumpers, and strangers who came in and settled down to a farm on the general presumption of their neighbors that they had shot an uncle or sired an untimely baby someplace in Tennessee or the Carolinas. I well remember (the week, by the way, that Truman fired MacArthur) sitting at the bedside of a very aged lady in Alpine, Texas. She would have been about ten or fifteen years Garner's senior, but she talked with that intense concreteness of the very old when they are recalling their childhood and youth. She talked about the feuding families and the silent types who settled in the Davis Mountains; and she spoke with contempt of an expansive jolly man who came through in the 1870s, was full of praise for the bare landscape and said he meant to settle there for the reason that he liked the people and thought it was great farming country. Evidently, he had not shot or ravished anybody. "From then on," said the old crone, "he was a suspicious character."

There was a lot of preaching on the frontier, but it was reserved for Sunday meeting and left to one man, a professional. By weekday, you dealt with your fellow man, agile fly-by-nights, and rustlers and crooked lawyers and people who poisoned crops and dynamited wells. And from time to time there was an Indian raid. One of the first cases tried by the twenty-five-year-old Garner, when he was a county judge, was a gang of men who had been systematically cutting down pasture fences. Barbed wire was a comparative novelty, an omen of the coming of law and order; it fenced off the open range and said, This land is mine. Marauders who liked to make the most of the chaos of the range burned pastures, cut the wire, and left warnings to anyone who replaced it. Garner, in this case, bypassed the finer points of the law. He simply turned the Texas Rangers on them.

In his early twenties, by 1890, Garner had moved four hundred and fifty miles southwest, but still in Texas, to Uvalde, which grows pecan nuts and harvests a fine crop of mohair from land that only a goat can thrive on. This was where John Nance Garner hung out his shingle as a lawyer. Pretty soon he was in the Texas legislature and in 1902 he went to Congress, a small farmer's, railroad-hating Populist who burrowed his way into power through the channels he knew best: the back room, the small office, the poker game, the little chat with worried men. All his life he distrusted orators, "crooners" as he used to call them. Politics was doing the best you could for the people you knew best; and that meant wheedling bills through a reluctant Congress. He was a tireless wheedler, and he once said that "a snort of bourbon is a better persuader than the Twelve Apostles." Whenever a sad man came to him complaining he was getting nowhere with a local bill he'd sworn to sponsor, Garner would shuffle him off to his small office. "Come," he'd say, "let's go and strike a blow for liberty."

Such new forces as organized labor were as strange to him as space men in science fiction. And labor reciprocated, in the words of the miners' John L. Lewis: "He is a poker-playing, whiskey-drinking, labor-baiting, evil old man." The vice president couldn't have cared less about this kind of attack. The vice presidency itself he thought a mistake, a highfalutin step into the robes of power, not power itself.

No other president and his vice president have spanned such a gamut in their upbringing, social status and experience of American life. Garner, dirt-poor in barren Texas, had, as a child, known a woman who had been scalped. His early staple diet was fat-back pork and watered rot-gut whiskey. And yet the grandeur of the vice presidency was not worth "a spit in a pot."

Roosevelt was such a precious young scion of the Hudson Valley squirearchy that his mother shielded him for as long as possible from association with such rough-hewn types as Ivy League teenagers. But once in politics, this legendary dude of the establishment soon learned that most political decisions in a democracy turn on the judgment of men (mostly) born closer to Garner's America than to FDR's. Roosevelt always confided his more romantic political fantasies to the wary mind of the man from the goat country. And when he was assailed and ridiculed for his lapse into the naïveté of proposing to retire all the Supreme Court justices over seventy and supplant them with six (!) true New Deal objectivists, FDR asked Garner what was likely to happen.

"D'you want it," queried Garner, "with the bark on or off?"

"Off!"

"Captain, you're beat."

Until he was ninety, Garner attributed his great age to bourbon and water, and then, when he was ninety-nine, to "layin' off" bourbon and water. The other night he took a fever, went into a coma, and died, on the verge of his hundredth year. I was about to say there is nobody left who is like him. There is one man. Lyndon Johnson is like him.

3

Frank Lloyd Wright

(1959)

I met him first on a winter's afternoon in what I almost slipped into calling the vestry of his suite at the Plaza Hotel in New York. I pressed the electric button at first timorously, then boldly, then incessantly, and was about to turn away when the door was opened by a pretty young woman, a secretary, or granddaughter, or vestal virgin perhaps, who beckoned me into the hushed gloom behind her through which I expected to see sacramental tapers. Then she nodded and vanished down the corridor.

It is difficult to avoid these liturgical images in introducing him because his reputation, his public pronouncements, his photographs—the majestic head, the marble serenity, the Miltonic collars, the cape of Superman—all conspired to suggest a sort of exiled Buddha, a high priest scuttled from his temple by the barbarians, one of those deposed monarchs so frequently seen around New York who gamely try to convey that a freewheeling democracy is just their speed. The room he sat in was seedy, in a lavish Edwardian way, and no single furnishing—no chair, fabric, window casement, carpet, lintel, or doorknob—appeared to have been invented much later than the June of 1867 in which he was born. He lay stretched out on a sofa, his fine hands folded on his lap, a shawl precisely draped around his shoulders.

He looked like Merlin posing as Whistler's Mother. Indeed, there was always a curiously feminine grace about him, but it was nothing frail or skittish. He looked more like a matriarch of a pioneer family, one of those massive western gentlewomen who shipped the piano from Boston round the Horn, settled in the Sacramento Valley, defied the Argonauts as they set fire to the cattle barns, and, having finally reclaimed their Spanish land grants, came into their own again as the proud upholders of old manners against the derision and ribaldry of the new rich.

In writing about him as a character delineated by Henry James, or sentimentalized by Gertrude Atherton, I hope that I am not so much arranging a suitable atmosphere as conveying a psychological shock. One expected a tyrant, a man constantly caricatured by the press as a bellowing iconoclast. And here was a genial skeptic whose habitual tone was one of pianissimo raillery.

It may be that I knew him too late, when the fire and brimstone were all spent, when whatever lava had been in him in the turbulent days had cooled and hardened in the enormous, firm dewlaps that started at his nostrils and seemed to be tucked away not far above the clavicle. There must be some explanation for the discrepancy between the legend and the man. Perhaps his long decade of neglect in his sixties, when he had to borrow from friends to retrieve a mortgage on his own home, is as good as any.

At any rate, all my apprehension vanished as he threw me, from a seniority of forty-odd years, the flattery of calling me "young man" and asking what was on my mind. It was a project that was to waver and die and come alive again in his eventual appearance on a television program. He dismissed it at once as an absurdity, since it involved a medium only slightly less debased than the movies. I told him that no sponsors would interrupt his sermon, the models he used would be of his own choosing, he could say exactly what he pleased.

He wafted the whole vision aside as a bit of vulgarity for which he would not hold me responsible. Then he slipped, from total and inexplicable free association, into a diatribe against Franklin Roosevelt. In some dim but infuriating way, Roosevelt, it seemed, was responsible for the triumph of the rabble, for the "agony of our cities, for skyscrapers, for the United Nations building ("an anthill for a thousand ants"), for the whole mushroom fashion of what he called "Nuremberg Fascist Modern," and for the coming destruction of the Edwardian pile we were sitting in ("the only beautiful hotel," he said bafflingly, "in all of this god-awful New York"). About two hours later, by which time he had murmured most of the slogans from his latest book, he chuckled and said: "Tell me, Alistair boy, did you ever meet an executive, a president of a corporation, a button-pusher, who had a smitch of aesthetic in his makeup?" I said I never had.

"Very well, then, when do you want me to appear and where?"

We blocked out the feature and arranged rehearsals, and went around for weeks in euphoria, which was shattered when he passed down an ultimatum through an emissary: "No rehearsals! Rehearsals freeze the natural flow of the human personality." This sounds awful in print, but all such sententiae were delivered, either in person or over the phone, in the delicate and warmly modulated voice which had for fifty years seduced wax manufacturers, oil tycoons, bishops, university boards of trustees, and at least one emperor of Japan into commissioning cantilevered Aztec structures most of which were later rescinded, condemned as unsafe, or merely paid for and deplored.

On the day of the show, we asked to pick him up after his midday nap and brought him to the studio well ahead of time. He had evidently forgotten all about the fiat against rehearsals, and stood by a model of his Bartlesville, Oklahoma, building and watched the stage manager chalk in a position for him on the floor. "What is this?" he asked, pointing down at the tiny prison yard he was meant to move in. I recalled to him the actor's famous crack about television ("Someone stuck in an iron lung") and he smiled and seemed to be pacified again. The director's voice came squawking over the loudspeaker: "Mr. Wright, will you turn and face the model?" He must have thought it was God's commandment, for he raised his head and said to the air the appalling syllable, "No."

He thereupon sauntered off to get his hat, cane, and cape. I chased him and got him off for a stroll around the dark cavern of the studio that lay beyond the lighted set. It was a tight moment. He needed to be coaxed, but he could spot a fawn at twenty paces, and flattery got you nowhere. We had only an hour to go, but he took my arm and we pattered in circles in the gloom while the director watched the minute hand of the clock. I agreed that television was a catch-as-catch-can business but suggested it was hardest of all on the cameramen, "the real craftsmen." I mentioned that they could not trust to luck, they had to block their shots and know where the prima donnas intended to move. Five minutes later, he was back on the set, as malleable as an aging cat. The scripted outline was forgotten. We simply sat and talked, and to comatose or apoplectic millions he trotted out such unashamed ad libs as: "The interior decorator is simply an inferior desecrator of the work of an artist"; "we are all victims of the rectangle and the slab, we go on living in boxes of stone and brick, while the modern world is crying to be born in the discovery that concrete and steel can sleep together"; "we should learn from the snail—it has devised a home that is both exquisite and functional."

After this first bout with the most highly advertised ego of our time I ran into him in various places or was asked to call on him, and I probably presume in saying that my failure to discern any conceit in him but only a harmless vanity, penetrating observation, and always his beautifully cadenced good sense was due to one of those accidents of personal chemistry that seal confidence in an instant and dissolve mountains of fear or antagonism that can never be argued away by two uncongenial people.

The last time I saw him, a year ago, I was to "moderate" a debate in Chicago on the present condition of our cities. The panel consisted of real estate men, a housing commissioner, a young professor of architecture, and Wright. It was sponsored by a steel company that legitimately hoped to popularize "the steel curtain," which is now the first constituent of most of the skyscrapers going up. Wright outraged his sponsors, and almost broke up the forum, first by professing boredom over the arguments of the buildings and real estate men and consequently walking out to take a nap; and later by indicating a diorama advertising the steel curtain and saying: "These steel frames are just the old log cabin, they are all built from the outside in, first a steel frame, then they bring in the paper hanger, and what have you got?—a box with steel for horizontals instead of lumber."

Driving back along the Chicago lakefront he had done most to glorify, he ridiculed the glinting skyscrapers and the whizzing automobiles ("rectangles on wheels"), but he could work up no steam or bile. His only genuine sigh was for the universal misuse of steel, "this beautiful material that spins like a spider and produces a tension so perfect that you can balance a monolith on a pinpoint." I felt that this lament of the city he secretly adored was a little recitation for Buncombe. In his ninetieth year, he could afford to be agreeable to everybody, though he tried valiantly to resist the inclination. After all, it had been forty-eight years since he had pioneered the sweeping horizontals of the first "prairie house" (which would pass creditably anywhere as a distinguished "contemporary" house), fifty-one years since he had built the first air-conditioned building, fifty-four years since the first metal-bound plate-glass door, forty-eight years since the cantilevered floor, poured concrete, and all the other explosive solecisms that are now the grammar of the modern architect.

One imagines him arriving this weekend in Heaven, tapping his malacca cane against the pearly gates to test the strength of the carbonate of lime and greeting Saint Peter with the disarming tranquil gaze and the snowy head held high. He will ask to see the "many mansions I've been hearing about for nearly ninety years," and will be taken on an obsequious tour only to discover, without surprise and without regret, that there is a distressing reliance on Gothic; that there is nothing so bold as the cantilevered balcony over the waterfall in Bear Run, Pennsylvania; that nothing has been done to dampen with colored glass the enormous glare of the light that never was on land or sea. He will say as he turns away in boredom from his guide: "The principle of floating all these structures on a more or less stable mass of cumulus clouds is no newer than the cushion of mud I put under the Imperial Hotel in Tokyo in 1922, with the express purpose of withstanding (as it did) the wrath of God. I understand He has been sulking ever since."

4

Wodehouse at Eighty

(1961)

[The Nazi invasion of France in the spring of 1940 did not ignore Wodehouse's house in the South. To his immense surprise, he was arrested and taken to Silesia, where he was kept as a prisoner of war for eighteen months, unaware of the disasters inflicted on the Lowlands, on beaten France, not least on his countrymen and -women in the Battle of Britain.

Just as he was due to be released, as a sixty-year-old, he was invited to do some broadcasts to America (not yet in the war) over the Nazi radio in Berlin. A political innocent all his life, and never more so than now, he readily agreed as a way, he said, of repaying his American readers and friends for their books, letters, and general concern for him.

Today, the broadcast scripts read as lighthearted accounts of prison life in a German rural town at any time in the twentieth century. But read by victims of Nazi saturation bombing they were an outrage and caused a furor in Britain. There was serious discussion

in the House of Commons of prosecuting Wodehouse for treason af-
ter the war. The uproar eventually died down, but he never again
went back to England.]

Long Island may fairly be seen as a fish nosing into the
North American mainland at Manhattan. At the tail end, a
hundred miles east into the Atlantic, there are two fins,
widely separated, which enclose the large Peconic Bay. The
north fin, called the North Fork, is inhabited by the survivors
of original Colonial settlers and by the descendants of early
twentieth century immigrant Poles, who are unpretentious,
hardworking, pure and good. The south fin, or Shore, is inhabited by the rich, the bad and the beautiful, since the Second World War especially by affluent stock manipulators,
television producers, interior decorators, actresses and their
preying ten percenters.

It is an unlikely place to find the Master of Jeeves. But he
lives a mile or two west of the bay, on the South Shore, in a
rural haven quite isolated from the pervasive smell of success. Remsenburg was named for one Joris Remsen, a Dutch-
man owning three spacious tracts of land in New York City
who, once the British had finally conquered and renamed
the city of New Amsterdam, decamped from its alien rule
and a small floodtide of arriving Englishmen. Remsen fled
eighty miles east and set up a small, bosky village which down
two centuries and more has become an oasis of well-spaced
houses and shade trees in the scrub-pine tundra on which
the nouveau Long Islanders have built, at ten-foot intervals,
their expensive variations of *ein bauhaus* by the sea.

Remsenburg is just about on the map and you have to watch out for narrow roads leading off the ocean highway and, after studying the instructions, pass a white wooden Colonial church and enter, at last, Basket Neck Lane.

It is an American lane, so there are no hedges, but the comfortable wooden houses lie back from the road on well-groomed lawns, and on the hot air of last Saturday afternoon a mower droned like a beehive. The houses have no names or numbers but only plaques propped against the entrance of the driveways. You go slowly down the lane and almost at its end see a privet hedge enclosing a wide lawn. This is the English touch. This must be it. Sure enough there is a small reflector sign against the hedge. It says "Wodehouse" and you lift your eyes from it and, as if this were the opening of a well-rehearsed television program, you "dolly up" to its owner, a big, pink, shambling, bald-headed man with thick glasses who is coming down the driveway and saying, "How nice of you to come, where shall we go? I think it might be cooler in the house."

He was right, for the Indian summer has burned like a crystal this last golden week or two, and so we went quickly over the lawn across a terrace, blinked at a circle of blinding white chairs and went into a wing of the house that turned out to be his study, overlooking a flaming maple and the small pines and locusts that abound on Long Island.

The second impression confirmed the first, which he had made over the telephone with a voice of extraordinary ease and tunefulness. It is an English voice, secure and genial, with a disarming air of wanting to help, meaning to find an agreeable time and place, not wanting to fuss. It is difficult to describe this voice, which is tuned entirely in C major. It is not, shall we say, a tune that you hear much in the chambers or the lounges of the United Nations.

Will you have a drink? It is a little early. Wouldn't it be better if we took off our coats? We drop them over a Chippendale chair. "Now," he says and puts his pipe in his mouth and gets up and down in the restlessness of the pipe-smoker's pursuit of the one match that will really work. This chase gives you time to focus his huge dumpling body, which is dressed in a long linen coat over a small-check sports shirt, fawn trousers, and canvas shoes with thick soles the color of almond icing. He is a giant Pickwick, an aging Micawber who had everything delightful turn up at once: good health ("a little hard of hearing in the left ear, that's all"), the ideal hermitage ("I love it here and go to New York only two or three times a year"), a happy marriage ("my goodness, it's been forty-seven years") and a sweet-flowing stream of filthy lucre ("I get an awful lot of money out of Sweden, I can't think why").

"Now," he said again, as his pipe wheezed a reedy bass against the melodic tenor of his voice. "Tell me, this is awfully exciting news that the *Guardian* is printing in London. Do you think it was wise to drop the name 'Manchester,' I wonder?"

I claimed the Fifth Amendment on that one and maneuvered, with astonishing lack of success, to get him off my job onto his. He kept springing up and down, moving piles of English newspapers and magazines still unwrapped, and occasionally disciplining a snuffling boxer that had appeared from nowhere and started to lick my nostrils and ears. "Is she being a nuisance?" It was nothing really, I assured him, and came up for air before Debbie, an ill-named hound, started on my teeth.

After about twenty minutes of praising and deploring the English newspapers ("they have the best and worst"), it was time to be firm with Debbie and with Pelham Grenville Wodehouse. Debbie had been joined by a dachshund, and they were both removed, and he beamed again in utter benevolence. Not quite utter, perhaps, for his thick circular lenses give him the slightest look of Dr. Mabuse.

After Le Touquet ("the house was completely smashed in the war") he lived in Paris for a while and in 1947 came back to America. In 1952 he and his wife were staying with his oldest friend and collaborator, Guy Bolton, "down here, and my wife came in from this awful jungle and she'd bought a house. It was a shack, but you see we fixed it up and built on to it, and reclaimed twelve acres from this scrub, and I don't think I shall ever leave Remsenburg." He is eighty on Sunday, and I smiled a salute at the gallantry of the word "ever."

I supposed that he had a host, at least a clutch, of close friends around. "No, no," he fluted, as if he was lucky to be so free of claims, "only Guy Bolton. You don't really need more than one, do you?" It was evidently enough for him. "Of course, I wave to the neighbors. They are very friendly and all that. But no friends, we never go to parties or travel anymore." He sounded like a TV announcer describing the halcyon life for a Florida insurance company.

When had he last been in England?

"I went over in nineteen-thirty-nine to see a cricket match.

It was between Dulwich and St. Paul's. It was very dull. T. Bailey played a dreadful innings. They tell me England has changed in many ways, but nobody can agree on what ways."

We were headed for another pleasant detour so I brought him back on the main road with perhaps a brutal bang.

"I think I'd better bring this up," I said, "because a lot of people do wonder about it. You saw the last piece by Evelyn Waugh about you and the Germans and those broadcasts during the war?"

He came over to a closer chair and bent down, his pink face suddenly quite intent and grave.

"Yes, I did."

"Does it make you feel relieved or embarrassed to have this thing thrashed over again?"

His pipe wheezed again, and wrinkled his features, if it's possible to wrinkle features as ripe and smooth as an apple.

"I don't know," he said, honestly baffled. "I wonder if it was necessary. Evelyn Waugh is such a fine friend. I've really been in two minds about it. What do you think?"

I told him as gently as possible that I thought it had done him a service, because scurrilous legends don't wither, "they simply get coarse and smelly, and someone comes along who knows no more about you than the obvious thing about Captain Boycott. They'd say 'Oh that Wodehouse, wasn't he mixed up somehow with the Nazis?'"

He was suddenly like a bishop who has heard an artless truth from the lips of a babe or suckling. "Yes," he said eagerly. "I think you're right. Yes, I see." He thought through a smoky pause. "Yes," he said, as if it was the last word. "I *am* grateful."

We started up again almost as if lunch or some other domestic entrant had intervened. I wanted to ask him about his daily routine, and the writing he was doing, but there was the awkward possibility that he might be doing very little and be too proud to say so, and I might clumsily invite him to admit that his day was done and his market gone with the wind, the Second War and the Welfare State. So I mentioned the "new book" *The Ice in the Bedroom* and the literary study of him *(Wodehouse at Work)* just coming out by a certain learned Usborne.

"Oh," he said, "the novel came out here last year. But the other book is a rather frightening thing, you know. I mean, I'm sure it's very conscientious and impressive to have someone go into one's stuff like that, but it's rather unsettling. I mean, you turn the stuff out and then public orators begin to declaim and critics analyze it . . . well, it's rather uncomfortable." He writhed with unaffected conviction.

"Do you find"—this was the sneaky foot in the door—"that people still *want* the stuff turned out? I understand you're translated all over."

"Well," he said, waving his pipe and stressing every other adjective, "it's the most *remarkable* thing. I don't believe there is a *single* language—wait now, I am not sure about the Russians—that hasn't translated it. I get books in Burmese and Korean and Japanese, and I can't think what they are. You have to trace them like hieroglyphs and read them backwards. And all the time, you wrote them. It's *most* amazing. I can't think what *they* think they're reading!"

His bewilderment seemed completely genuine, and through all our talk there was the novel feeling that here was a hermit, a recluse, a sort of musical comedy Schweitzer, who had honestly no idea that he'd ever been heard of, or read outside the dormitories of English public schools when the lights were out. The calls from American magazines and agents (it was coming out now) of course were understandable. "They go on and on. I just had a call from an agent who wants me to make a musical comedy out of Barrie's *The Admirable Crichton*. And then they're well along with a series of television shows about Jeeves. But I don't understand the other countries. The Communists, for instance. There was a ban on me in Hungary for a while, which is just as mysterious as their reading me at all. But they do. The Czechs and the Poles and the rest. Perhaps they think of me as a satirist."

He chuckled over this and added in a confessional tone. "Of course, I've always gone rather on the assumption that country houses and butlers have never passed away."

I thought of Margaret Fuller accepting the universe and said mildly, "You'd better. After all, it's your staple."

"Of course it is," he cried, grateful for the *mot juste*. "It's my staple. I don't pretend these things exist. They probably never have existed. They're really historical novels. I suppose there are no Bertie Woosters, at least, anymore. If there are, I imagine they're on the make. You see, I do feel we have lost something, even in the crooks and bounders. The Woosters were really innocent people. That's what we've lost—innocence."

This led by an obvious but gloomy association to the modern comedians and humorists. In the only downright sentence he ever spoke, he said he disliked the "sick" comedian. He writhed a little and found a better word.

"Geniality," he said, "I think that's what I miss in the new comics and the humorists."

I wondered who the new humorists were, and he wondered too. "Really, when you come to think of it, I can't think of any young ones coming along except Jean Kerr. When I first came to this country, everybody was funny, the writers, the vaudeville comics, the iceman, the neighbors. . . ."

Couldn't this have been the delight of a first exposure to the oblique turn of American minds?

"Maybe, maybe," he said, making another tremendous discovery. "But there are no more Benchleys and Thurbers, and George Ades or S. J. Perelmans, or in England any more W. W. Jacobs and Barry Paines. And Nunnally Johnson, now there was a fine humorist." He remembered a story of Johnson's about a man who used to come home every day and find that his wife had moved the furniture around. One day he came home and flung himself on the bed, but the bed wasn't there. So there was a court case and she was sued. He told his story "and every man in the court had gone through the same thing. The case was dismissed. Now there, you see, no magazine would possibly take that today."

We were on the dangerous ground where a younger man suggests that maybe humor dates more than most forms of literature. Also, Debbie or the dachshund was snuffling and scratching at the door. So I came finally to the mystery of this exile and this hermitage.

"Tell me," I said, "don't you find it difficult to mine your stuff at three thousand miles from its source?"

"Ah," he said (the Geiger counter was swiveling like mad

45

now), "I've had misgivings about that from time to time. But you see, even when I lived in England, I only went to country houses till I got the feel of what it was all about." He rested the hand with the pipe on one knee. "You know, I've always been a recluse. I've never seen any sort of life—*I got it all from the newspapers!*"

So, the rich and deathless population of Wodehouse County is all a fantasy. It struck me that to the extent his picture of country house life is imagined, it probably crystallizes, better than any enlargement of reality, the preconceptions of the foreigner, especially of the Communists, who must at this moment be learning the dreadful truth about the West by commuting between *Leave It to Psmith* and *Little Dorrit* in order to strike the proper balance between the life of the oppressors in their castles and the oppressed in their factories. He thought it very likely.

The dogs bounded in again and converged on my French poodle, which had broken out of the car. There was an ugly snarl and yelp or two, and the talk was plainly at an end. "Debbie, Debbie," he said, almost weeping with affection over this slobbering monster of a boxer. "Gently, gently." He picked her up and saw me across the lawn and down the driveway. With the free hand he waved, as to a neighbor, and padded out of the burning sun and back into the shade of the house and the real world of Psmith and Jeeves and Lord Emsworth and Mr. Mulliner and Bertie Wooster, who don't exist any more except in the puzzled but fascinated imaginations of about eighty or ninety nations.

5

FDR

(1999)

My first memory of President Roosevelt in the flesh was at the three hundredth anniversary of the founding of Harvard College, a weeklong celebration in September 1936. Roosevelt was to be the main speaker in the closing ceremony. But the whole affair was such a dazzling circus of exhibitions (manuscripts, antiquities), symphony concerts, torchlight parades, fireworks—all staged for the first and surely last convention of world scholarship—that it was enough to obliterate in retrospect the sharp memory of all the participants—all except one. It was my first reporting assignment for a newspaper, for anybody, and it was a daunting initiation.

Over seven hundred eminent scholars from forty-two foreign universities had been invited on terms that can be said to be uniquely demanding if not outrageously rude: that they should turn in to the president of Harvard the results of orig-

49

inal—and hitherto unpublished—research carried out during the previous two years. Most of these papers were so specialized, so beyond the intellectual range of the reporters present, that we simply had to note and take on trust the vital importance of Professor Millikan's cosmic ray researches, the excursions of Sir Arthur Eddington into the interior of the stars, Dr. Howard Northrop's meditations on the formation of enzymes. The uncomprehending majority of reporters present were left to grab a one-day sensation out of the discovery of Dr. Friedrich Bergius of Heidelberg of how to convert wood into carbohydrates. It offered a startling piece on the grim prospect of a besieged nation at war being adequately fed on sawdust.

When the final day came, the delegates discovered that President Conant was about to confront them with something not at all entertaining and far more challenging than anything they had seen all week (perhaps, for some of them, all their lifetime). It was to hear four famous men, two from democracies, two from totalitarian regimes, express themselves on an idea: the idea of Freedom.

The most eminent living anthropologist, Bronislaw Malinowski, was the first to speak for our side: "Our present civilization is passing through a very severe, perhaps a crucial, stage of maladjustment. The abuse of legal and administrative power; the inability to create lasting conditions of peace; the recrudescence of aggressive militarism" (no mention of passive militarism!); "the torpor of true religion and the assumption of religious garb by doctrines of racial or national superiority or the gospel of Marx . . . it is our duty to insist on the necessity for freedom." This was all impressively high-toned but once the echoes of its eloquence had faded, much of it was seen to be begging the question. "The inability to create lasting conditions of peace" is not a twentieth-century failing: it was demonstrated so long ago as 1307 by the brave Pierre Dubois, legal adviser to the king of France, and the organizer of the first league of nations. And to whom shall we present our "insistence" on "the necessity of freedom"? Adolf Hitler? Neville Chamberlain?

In response came two scholars of world renown, from Rome and Tokyo. Dr. Corrado Gini, professor of sociology at the University of Rome, didn't even begin to dispute "the necessity for freedom"; plainly, to him, it was a naive delusion of people who had no historical perspective. To every nation, he granted, "there must be an appropriate" alternation of "tension and relaxation of authority." While admitting the "wisdom" of some liberal eras, he yet believed that "Italy today requires a Fascism." So there!

There was even less hope of a workable formula for compromise between tense and relaxed authority from the great Masaharu Anesaki, professor of religion in the University of Tokyo. The very notion of freedom, he casually implied, is irrelevant to the spiritual well-being of a nation. He simply saw "the modern civilization of the West as a power working for its own destruction . . . a power civilization impotent to overcome, and unfit to be totally absorbed in, the" presumably superior "spiritual heritage of the East."

At last, or next to the last, came the man whom this theme had obsessed for the past two years. The president of Harvard himself: James B. Conant. Not physically a heroic figure, a small, thin, bespectacled clerky type, not unlike a comic strip stereotype of a "professor." But he was the man who had stood up against the Massachusetts legislature and its urge to enforce a loyalty oath on teachers throughout the state, and on this last day, he was the most impressive figure. Now his lean voice pierced through the rising wind and the restless audience: "In the name of Harvard," he proclaimed, "one essential condition for the continuance of a national culture: *absolute* freedom of discussion, *absolutely* unmolested inquiry."

Even so general a plea was about to receive a practical test from fifteen thousand Harvard men who had passed around the Yard. The coming main speaker would soon stand there and require tolerance and silence from an audience to possibly fifty percent of whom his views were monstrous and heretical.

That left, however, fifty percent who never went to Harvard, townspeople who had spent weeks scrambling for a ticket to the Yard and this famous occasion. They were beginning to thrash their arms against the cold and crane their heads to catch the first glimpse of the star turn, when the gray sky blackened and a sudden billow of wind from the east brought on a torrent of rain and drove everybody indoors. Not quite everybody. Probably less than a third of the expectant crowd could jam into the Sanders Theatre, and it took time till they were packed to the windowsills. The thousands who couldn't make it stayed huddled outdoors, their drenched ears cocked for the hero. Inside, at last, the old ex-president Lowell fairly bellowed into the microphone: "Gentlemen, the president of the United States!" There were many old Harvard men quite prepared to boo or hiss. They were sufficiently well-bred, however, to sit on their hands. But no dissenting gesture short of a gunshot could have arrested the roar that for five clocked minutes rocked the theater and thundered out of the loudspeakers of a continent.

Through this sustained din, he came on slowly as the platform guests parted for him: leaning on an arm, the other hand clutching a cane, walking very slowly and straight-legged. "Seems," remarked one young student without guile or second thought, "to have trouble walking."

It was an artless remark but it was a taproot for me into the one visual memory of that day that remains indelible. For I have to confess that all the foregoing reportage and Roosevelt's lilting but unremarkable speech hoping "Harvard and America" would "stand for the freedom of the human mind" spring not from my memory but from a rescued photostat of my dispatch (September 20, 1936) to the London *Observer.*

Well before the final ceremony I had gone to the Yard expecting to flash my press credentials and be led down to the press rows by some marshal or usherette. But the main entrance was jammed with a dense, jostling crowd. I knew the Yard well (I had been at Harvard, after all, for a whole year) and I remembered a side entrance round a long curving wall. It was there all right, an open iron gate leading into a small yard not much larger than a capacious alley. Opposite the entrance gate was a door, which led through to the Yard.

But I had barely walked into the alley when there was the sudden swishing of a large automobile, a squawk of brakes and a rapid patter of footsteps running toward me. They belonged to a young bareheaded man in a suit who had one hand stuck in his right coat pocket. He was what I was to come to know well: a Secret Service man. He stopped me, pushed me, gently I must say, against a side wall and wondered what I was doing there. I showed him my credentials and was plainly so scared and innocent of all foul designs that I said I surely would stay unmoving against the wall until "the president has gone up to the Yard and we're out of here." The president! I had hardly time to pronounce the tremendous word than my man darted across the alley, opened the car door, and from the other side appeared two other men (during the Second War, it would always be one Secret Service man, one marine, and Elliott, Roosevelt's eldest son). They together made several swift and inexplicable passes, like jugglers, toward someone inside the car, and on a count (of three, I suppose) one cried "Now" and they lifted and held aloft a massive human figure crumpled into a squatting position, since one man had his arm crooked under the figure's knees, and the other under his upper back. It was Franklin Roosevelt, as inert as a sack of potatoes. His head could move and did so as he acknowledged the motions of the third man, who had dived into the car and emerged with a cane and a hat. Roosevelt was then deposited on the ground, his back straightened, the cane was put into his right hand, the hat stuck on his head. With a tug or two from his helpers, he braced himself, linked arms with one

54

man and limped stiff-legged toward the side entrance door and onto—I learned later—one of the ramps that were built in any public place with steps he was due to visit.

All this happened in much less time than it takes to tell, a trauma with two strokelets: the first registering the name— the president of the United States! The second, that he was a cripple. The president of the United States was a paraplegic!! It is something everybody in the world knows now though our not knowing it is disbelieved by succeeding generations who have seen the Roosevelt family's home movies and documentaries based on, no less, the whole history of his affliction. Yet if, at almost any time during the twelve years of Roosevelt's presidency, you had put the bare question ("Did you know that the president is a cripple?") I'm pretty sure that most of the population would have said something like, "I heard he had poliomyelitis at one time." But since the first fatal attack in 1921, he was never filmed for movie theater newsreels (there was, of course, no television throughout his lifetime) or ever photographed by news reporters in his wheelchair. This taboo was observed for twenty-five years— even by the press chains, like Hearst's, that hated him— throughout his governorship of New York State and throughout the four terms of his presidency. It is, I should think, a unique example of voluntary restraint. The result of it was to confirm triumphantly the psychologist's old discovery that the thing *seen* very soon obliterates the thing heard or read. That explained why the vast majority of the American population never thought of Roosevelt as a cripple. What, for a quarter century, was impressed on everyone's senses was the powerful upper body, the bull neck, the strong hands clasping the lectern, the handsome head tossing the spoken emphases, the happy squire waving to everybody from an open car, the perpetual optimist and Savior of America in the darkest days. So, though most people could accept the reminder, if ever it came up, that the president was paralyzed, it was a truth buried deep at the back of the mind.

As for the taboo that kept it there, a taboo that was faithfully observed by the national press for over twelve years, it is inconceivable that today it would be maintained for a week or a day. Some British tabloid would be sure to offer a fortune to the first to break it.

The sharpness of this memory obviously prejudiced me in his favor when, in the spring of 1937, I came as a news correspondent to Washington fresh from England, to report on the man who by then was a beacon to the peoples of the European countries that had not lost their liberties to Hitler on the rampage or foaming Mussolini or the man of steel (Stalin) in the Kremlin. In England, which I knew best, the old still lived with the memories of the enormous slaughter on the Western Front, and the young found little inspiration in a Tory government on the defensive moving backward, one step at a time, before Hitler's oncoming shadow. To many of the idealistic young, though, there was a rousing alternative to stomping Fascism and defensive Toryism. The public face of Communism in the Soviet Union had been so brightly painted by an older generation of early believers—

Shaw and Lady Astor and the Webbs among them—and the private terror by which the system worked was so well disguised or disbelieved that "to each according to his needs, from each according to his ability" seems a positively Christian doctrine.

But for the undifferentiated mass of still-free, self-governing Europeans, there was yet another exhilarating choice, and, across the Atlantic, Franklin Roosevelt was the heroic cast of it. To a Europe bereft of notable leaders who were not tyrants, here was a man who, defying the current totalitarian models and denouncing them, was reinvigorating the largest democracy by democratic means and with the enthusiastic consent of the mass of his people. What Europeans didn't know, or didn't care, was that Roosevelt had been able to exert a power usually prohibited by law to leaders in a democracy. He had demanded in his first inaugural speech powers beyond the restraints of the Constitution "if the normal balance of Executive and Legislative authority" did not prove "wholly adequate"; then "I shall ask the Congress for broad Executive power . . . as great as the power that would be given me if we were, in fact, invaded by a foreign foe." As he spoke those alarming words, he was already exercising extraordinary executive power: he had closed all the nation's banks, and *he* would decide which ones were to survive and which would go under. And the Congress, as fearful as the rest of the country of widespread civil disorder, gladly gave him the dictatorial powers he wanted, and America took its first fling at National Socialism. It was not at the time recognized as such. With a cheering smile, an open checkbook, and a logo (a blue eagle symbolizing the NRA—the National Recovery Administration), Roosevelt appropriated the law-making power, suspended the antitrust laws and set up what amounted to government by trade association. Employers were required to bind themselves to a code that fixed prices and wages and labor practices for about seven hundred industries, from the steel makers to the humblest commercial theatre. (I saved for many years the NRA code as it applied to all burlesque companies, solemnly setting the maximum wage for first banana, second banana, star stripper and so on.)

The honeymoon of America's benevolent dictator lasted for just over two years, when, after disputing an oil case and the sale-of-a-chicken case, the nine old men of the Supreme Court found the whole NRA codemaking authority "flagrantly unconstitutional."

Having given big business more than its due in running the country, he now turned to elevate the status and define new rights for the labor unions and the farmers, and embarked on the consummate political act of his career, assembling a vast, shambling but dependable, coalition of the unlikeliest allies. This ever-smiling, confident patrician—the very patent of good breeding and a gentlemanly conscience—never had a second's hesitation in making up to anyone he needed: rough labor leaders here, wily southern conservative senators there, the dictator of Louisiana, the men who ran corrupt city governments (in Chicago, Memphis, Jersey City). They were powerful and they could deliver the Democratic vote.

Many times in press conferences, and on the last two presidential campaigns, I came to marvel at the ease, the beautifully played cool, of his behavior to us, the press, the morning after a congressional defeat, a jolt from the Supreme Court. The secret spring of this ease and seeming indifference to the mounting criticism of the press and the hatred of him by the Republicans was his deep, undisturbable sense of what the mass of the people wanted. Not, as in Winston Churchill's liberal period, when he was appalled at poverty and wanted to return the poor to the decent estate to which God had ordered them. Roosevelt truly felt from the first to the last days in the White House that, after the degrading plunge into the Depression, everybody wanted not a return to the status quo ante but a better life altogether. He was so sure of the rightness of this instinct that he could toss off a defeat like a common cold. He had a new idea every day. As a testy columnist put it: "He started giving people federal money . . . to dig a ditch across Florida and build a dam to harness the tides of Fundy. The ditch and dam seemed not so good once they were under way; so, all right, skip them, and how about a new kind of Supreme Court?" This same columnist, an artful juggler with the English language, one Westbrook Pegler, paid Roosevelt the ultimate compliment, all the truer for coming from a man who for all of FDR's later years harbored an almost pathological hatred of him: "Never in our time have people been so conscious of the meanness which a complacent upper class will practice on the help, and of the government's duty to do something real and personal for the assistance of those who are so far down that they can't help themselves. . . . He needs to be fought all the time . . . but if the country doesn't go absolutely broke in his time, it will be a more intelligent and a better country after him."

Not long after I settled in here as a foreign correspondent, I came, like the Americans I lived and mingled with, to forget all about Roosevelt's affliction. Only from time to time did the memory float up as a question: by what miraculous inner drive could this cripple undertake the prodigious business of pulling American up by its shoddy shoes from the depths of despair and misery? (I had seen lots of both in two long drives across the country in 1933 and 1934, and was constantly amazed and relieved that there had been no outbreak of the threatened revolution.) And often in the Oval Office, I admired the marvelously assumed ease and casualness after some stunning blow, as at his press conference on the Tuesday, two days after Pearl Harbor, when he alone knew the shattering damage to the Pacific fleet (five battleships sunk or disabled, fourteen other ships, a hundred and twenty aircraft destroyed, two thousand seamen and four hundred civilians killed).

We did not know until Roosevelt had died, in April 1945, how distraught and disoriented he had been, how mortally sick, for the last year of his life. We never knew for twenty more years until Churchill's doctor published a diary that during the three and a half years when Roosevelt and Churchill were companions in arms, and during which Churchill had borne responsibility for the daily operations of every theater of the war, that Churchill had suffered one serious heart attack, three pneumonias, two strokes, an abdominal operation, hernia, deafness, an intractable skin disease, eye trouble and innumerable minor ailments.

That these two great men and chronic invalids should, more than any other two humans, have run and won the war for us is a mystery that, as Dr. Buechner might say, "some people call luck, some coincidence, and some call the grace of God."

6

Maker of a President:
Eleanor Roosevelt
(1962)

Mrs. Franklin D. Roosevelt, the widow of the thirty-second president of the United States, died last week in New York City where she was born seventy-eight years ago. Except for increasing deafness in old age, she had never been troubled with anything much more bothersome than a cold or a broken ankle until she took to a hospital bed a few weeks ago with a pestiferous condition that was eventually diagnosed as anemia complicated by a lung infection. "Eleanor," Franklin Roosevelt used to say, watching her and her notebook whirl continuously around the United States to check on soil erosion, unemployment, sick leave among nurses, or silicosis among miners, "has time for everybody's troubles but her own."

It was a proud complaint which, in the missionary days of the New Deal, the newspaper cartoonists turned into a national joke. Until Mrs. Roosevelt, First Ladies were supposed to be the most gracious furnishing of the White House. They kept the silver polished and the fires burning against the unpredictable return of the great man from the crushing appointments of his office. It is a tradition honored up to 1933 and since 1945. The twelve intervening years turned the White House into a sort of national hotel operation under emergency conditions. Protocol was packed off with the bags of Mr. and Mrs. Hoover. The president's bedroom was invaded at breakfast by the Brain Trust. Lunch was a sandwich on a tray dispensed to visiting governors, labor leaders, national committeemen. Birthdays, national holidays, and most Sunday evenings were the occasion of the famous and inedible Roosevelt buffets.

This genial chaos was the logical extension, on a national scale, of the domestic free-for-all which Franklin and Eleanor Roosevelt had developed at Hyde Park and Campobello, and at their house in New York, as the boisterous childhood of five children coincided with the effort of Mrs. Roosevelt and Louis Howe to boost her paralyzed husband into national politics and to save him from the fate which his mother prescribed with such grim resolve: "My son must come home to live in Hyde Park: he's going to be an invalid the rest of his life and he needs rest and complete quiet."

Even now, forty-one years after the famous chill at Campobello and the black two years during which Roosevelt agonized over the hardest task of a lifetime ("trying to move one toe"), the transformation of Franklin and Eleanor Roosevelt from an upper-class couple of no particular personal distinction into two iron characters who have left their permanent brand on history appears to be nothing less than a human miracle.

Eleanor's childhood and youth seemed a pathetic prelude to a life of social martyrdom. Her father was a gallant drunk, her mother the spoiled and beautiful daughter of a beauty more petulant still. She was a nuisance and butt. From earliest girlhood her mother mocked her for her gravity, her prominent teeth and shapeless mouth. She comforted herself in her journal with the thought that "no matter how plain we may be, if we have virtue and trust, they will show in our faces." She went to work in a settlement house and came to know the daily aspect of poverty, a running sore on the body politic that astonished and embarrassed Franklin.

Then came New York State politics in Albany, and the dreadful summer, and the dedicated battle with his mother, and soon his discovery that if he listened more and tossed his head less, he could like people and they could like him. Eleanor took night classes in government and sociology and fed her lessons to Franklin, while Louis Howe massaged his legs for hours on end. It is the symbolic picture of the rest of their lives. In the White House, when the steel braces grew too heavy, he took them off and Eleanor, fresh from the Midwest or the Deep South, read over the compassionate statistics she learned on the road with such unflagging and humorless devotion.

"The concept of duty," writes her biographer, "was Victorian, soft-headed, and entirely un-American, in the brassy 1920s. But Eleanor Roosevelt had it and it guided her entire existence." It transmuted an ugly duckling school-ma'am into a great woman, and it planed away the emotional fat in a feckless, generous man, knotted his fiber, and produced a great president. There are few women in the history of great nations who could claim such a personal achievement, and none less likely to make the claim. The people, though, sensed it and year after year, to the annoyance of her chuckling detractors, she was voted, in a national poll, the First Lady of the World.

For herself she simply listed in the *Who's Who* entry only three or four offices she filled on her own account. She might have recorded the sum of her great life with nothing more than her vital statistics and the single entry: "Created the thirty-second president of the United States."

7

General Marshall

(1959)

It has been a habit of these letters to honor, as W. H. Auden put it, "the vertical man," the Americans in all their variety who are up and doing. But Americans themselves are great celebrators of their eminent dead. And when the calendar reminds us of a great one who was born or died fifty or a hundred years ago, he is obediently honored in the tomb by people who would have feared or hated him in the flesh. For Americans, an impetuous but ceremonial people, are soon ready to pay tribute to a man once the wind is out of him.

Lately we observed as a holiday the date kept aside as Columbus Day, which celebrates the discovery of this country by a man who neither discovered it nor ever saw it. And a few days later we nodded respectfully in the direction of Harpers Ferry, West Virginia, where—a hundred years ago—John Brown, a near-lunatic with a hot eye and a single purpose, started on his wild and brief campaign to set up a free state in the Appalachians as a sanctuary for escaped Negro slaves. Next day, a man died who had been born just across the Pennsylvania border from Harpers Ferry who had an equally single purpose but who was so prosaic, so deeply disdainful of drama and public exposure, that not one American in a million would have recognized him on the streets, and not even his close friends knew a pungent or delightful story about him. He was almost impossible for a newspaperman to know, for he winced at the word "newspaper" and he therefore acquired no public personality, not even a couple of identifying adjectives in *Time*. In the last few years of his life he used to drive downtown most days from his small house in Pinehurst, North Carolina, buy his groceries in the supermarket, tote them to his car to the accompaniment of a nod from the townspeople, a bit of gossip with the drugstore clerk, and then get into his car again, receive the flourish of a salute from the traffic cop, and drive home again. Yet on a bright day, wherever in the world the American flag flies, it was lowered and flown for him.

I hope I won't be misunderstood if I say that he was a most un-American figure because he was so remarkably self-effacing. The United States has as many people as anybody afflicted with self-effacement, but it usually springs from social discomfort, or genuine shyness, or that other form of shyness which, as somebody wisely said, is a sure sign of conceit. This man was not shy, but the subordination of self to teamwork was almost an instinct with him, and I suppose few men who take to soldiering took to it for a better reason. Most Americans were willing to credit the reports of his eminence but it was something they had to take on trust; for General George Catlett Marshall, of all the great figures of our time, was the least "colorful," the least impressive in a casual meeting and the least rewarding to the collector of anecdotes. He was a man whose inner strength and secret humor only slowly dripped through the surfaces of life, as a stalactite hangs stiff and granity for centuries before one sees beneath it a pool of still water of marvelous purity.

He was always uncomfortable when anyone mentioned the great plan that bears his name, the plan to repair the fabric of European life after the devastation of the Second War. He took no credit for it, and he was nearly right. For it was first conceived by underlings in the State Department and seized on by Undersecretary Dean Acheson when he realized that all the largesse of UNRRA and Breton Woods, and the loan to Britain, and other loans to Greece and Turkey, were far from enough. It was time to jettison Europe or to throw out a lifeline. Acheson developed the plan, and it was worked on in the White House, and he floated it as a trial balloon in a speech at Cleveland, Mississippi. No one in the country took particular notice of it. Marshall had been in Europe and when he came back, Acheson told him about it, not without misgiving, for Americans had not marveled at his trial balloon, and a sudden Communist stab at Hungary might puncture it once and for all. Marshall, it must be said, now saw the necessity of speed and a public forum and contrived within two days to speak at the Harvard commencement. He was no orator, and the dramatic novelty of the plan went unnoticed by everybody except a trio of British correspondents and the

British foreign secretary, Ernest Bevin, who sat by his bedside in England and heard a transatlantic broadcast and responded to it at once as "a lifeline to sinking men . . . the generosity of it was beyond our belief . . . we grabbed it with both hands." So it is not for the Marshall Plan that we honor the general.

Imagine now a sturdy, well-knit man, stiff-necked it would be fair to say, certainly in the physical sense, with sandy hair and mild blue eyes and a homely, underslung mouth from which issued unspectacular remarks in a throaty voice. A student of war, from the books and the maps but also from the arms contracts and the quartermaster records, and from a personal knowledge of the battlefields picked up on private walks when the bones of the dead were long overgrown.

It is possible—we shall never know—that in his private imagination he was another Robert E. Lee who dreamed dreams of high deeds in the cannon's mouth. But for almost fifty years he was fated by his superiors and, in the crisis of his career, by his own conscience to return as always to the drawing board, to revise the training methods of a tank corps, to compute the comparative tactical efficiency of a 55 mm machine gun in close combat and in desert warfare, to gauge the competing need for antiaircraft of the slums of Chungking or the docks and ports of Iceland. A high subordinate who worked with him assures me that in the history of warfare Marshall could not have had his equal as a master of supply: the first master, as this West Point colonel put it, of global warfare. I suppose we must defer to this expert judgment. It was enthusiastically seconded by the three or four senior

British generals during the Second War. But to most of us, unifying the command of an army outpost or totting up the number of landing barges that could be spared from Malaya for the Normandy landings is hardly so flashing as Montgomery's long dash through the desert, or MacArthur's vigil on Bataan, or even the single syllable by which General McAuliffe earned his immortality: "Nuts!"

A layman is not going to break out a flag for a man who looks like a stolid golf-club secretary, a desk general who refused an aide-de-camp or a chauffeur and worked out of an office with six telephones. Even though 1984 comes closer every day, this is not yet an acceptable recipe for a hero. Though no doubt when Hollywood comes to embalm him on celluloid, he will grow a British basso, which is practically a compulsory grafting process for American historical characters in the movies. He will open letters with a toy replica of the sword of Stonewall Jackson (who was, to be truthful, a lifetime's idol).

But in life no such color brightened the gray picture of a man devoted to the daily study of warfare on several continents with all the ardor of a certified public accountant. In a word, he was a soldier's soldier. Nor, I fear, is there any point in looking for some deep and guilty secret to explain his reputation for justice and chivalry. There is, however, one voice that has been silent. No syllable of praise or criticism has come from a soldier who can coin resounding epitaphs when he so chooses. General MacArthur has said nothing, and I dare to wonder about his silence only because it reflects a conflict of character and temperament that was conducted

on both sides with shattering dignity. It will by now be no surprise to learn that on Marshall's side it was a most undra-
matic quality: the gift of making at fateful times sensible
decisions that elevate another man and swing the spotlight
away from you.

We have to go back to February 1956 for the last public
word about Marshall written by General MacArthur. "General Marshall's enmity towards me," he wrote, "was an old
one." Discounting the word "enmity," let us say that the original row—the sort of thing that elephants and politicians
never forget—goes back to the First World War, when Marshall, a colonel on the Operations Planning Section of the
American Expeditionary Force, was planning the recapture
of Sedan, the historic town which three German armies in
the last century have broken through to lay waste the lands of
France. Marshall's plans did not allow for the impetuous ambition of a young brigadier general to summon his own division and take Sedan at a bound. The brigadier general was,
need I say, MacArthur. He leaped through a loophole in the
Marshall Plan and took Sedan in his dashing stride. From
then on he vaulted ahead of Marshall in everything but pru-
dence. By 1930, when he became chief of staff, you would
have had to scan the army lists with binoculars to see what
happened to Marshall.

After the First War, you might have thought that his appearance at the side of General Pershing as a personal aide
would have assured a flashier or more enterprising type
some quick preferment, but it was downhill again for another fifteen years. As late as 1933, for instance, he was ap-

pointed senior instructor to the Illinois National Guard, an appointment that would have thrilled a scoutmaster. But for an able soldier, fifty-two years of age, it was the pit of his career. Once MacArthur retired, in 1935—and it may be no more than coincidence—Marshall had his feet on the ladder again. Two days before the Germans swept into Poland he was made chief of staff.

I said that in the supreme crisis of his career it was his own conscience that sent him back to the commanding obscurity that was his habitat. Nobody has told this incident better than the late Henry Stimson, Roosevelt's secretary of war. In a letter to the president in August 1943, Stimson wrote, "I believe the time has come when we must put our most commanding soldier in charge of this critical operation [that was to be the invasion of Europe]. You are far more fortunate than was Mr. Lincoln or Mr. Wilson in the ease with which that selection can be made. . . . General Marshall already has a towering eminence of reputation as a tried soldier and as a broad-minded and skillful administrator." The British had, in fact, suggested him. Churchill assumed he was already picked and Stalin had vouchsafed a wily nod of approval. There came a day in Cairo when President Roosevelt and Marshall lunched alone. It seems to be accepted among Marshall's close friends that he had all his life yearned for a combat command. The most majestic command in history was his for the asking. Roosevelt had already made up his mind but, as usual, allowed himself room to maneuver (and lament) if things didn't turn out his way. He asked Marshall whether he would prefer to stay in Washington as chief of staff or take the supreme command. Stimson kept some notes, made from Roosevelt's account of the lunch, and in them he says that Marshall declined the gambit. It was, he said, entirely for the president to decide. He warned the president that if he was chosen to go to Europe, there was only one man he could think of to replace him in Washington. It was the new general Dwight D. Eisenhower, who had commanded the North African landings. The president decided that Eisenhower had neither Marshall's grasp of worldwide strategy nor his familiarity with Congress. So he picked Eisenhower, and Marshall congratulated him, and the lunch was over. At the end of it, Roosevelt said, "I couldn't sleep nights, George, if you were out of Washington." (Roosevelt is the only known man who ever called General Marshall "George.") When Stimson heard of this he was, he said, "staggered." He gave to his diary the note that "at the bottom of his heart it was Marshall's secret desire above all things to command the invasion of Europe." But Marshall himself had advanced the deciding argument. Who else would oversee the war of supply, who would review the war in both oceans, from the necessary desk in Washington? He never by any sign showed that the president's decision was not the perfect one. The British too were staggered and apprehensive, and it was a British official who put down in *his* journal: "In Marshall's presence ambition folds its tent." Stimson put down an older sentence he had once quoted about Marshall: "He that ruleth his spirit is better than he that taketh a city."

When the dust and the glory came blowing up over the battlefields, Marshall was the father confessor and guru to

Eisenhower. To MacArthur he was still a sullen office figure, smarting at long range over the humiliation at Sedan, but it was Marshall who urged on Congress the award to MacArthur of the Medal of Honor. Twelve years later, when Eisenhower was campaigning for the presidency in Wisconsin, he deleted—at the personal urging of Governor Kohler, of Senator McCarthy's Wisconsin—a passage in praise of Marshall from a speech that he was about to give. Not a word ever passed the lips of Marshall about this dismal episode, and when McCarthy called him a traitor for the failure of his postwar mission to China, all Marshall said to a personal friend was: "The hardest thing I ever did was to keep my temper at that time."

There is a final story about him which I happen to have from the only other man of three present. I think it will serve as a proper epitaph. In the early 1950s, a distinguished, a very lordly, American magazine publisher badgered Marshall to see him on what he described as a serious professional mission. He was invited to the general's summer home in Virginia. After a polite lunch, the general, the publisher, and the third man retired to the study. The publisher had come to ask the general to write his war memoirs. They would be serialized in the magazine and a national newspaper, and the settlement for the book publication would be handsome indeed. The general instantly refused on the grounds that his own true opinion of several wartime decisions had differed from the president's. To advertise the difference now would leave Roosevelt's defense unspoken and would imply that many lives might have been saved. Moreover, any honest account might offend the living men involved and hurt the widow and family of the late president. The publisher pleaded for two hours. "We have had," he said, "the personal testaments of Eisenhower, Bradley, Churchill, Stimson, James Byrnes. Montgomery is coming up, and Alanbrooke, and yet there is one yawning gap." The general was adamant. At last, the publisher said, "General, I will put it on the line. I will tell you how essential we feel it is to have you fill that gap, whether with two hundred thousand words or ten thousand. I am prepared to offer you one million dollars after taxes for that manuscript." General Marshall was faintly embarrassed, but quite composed. "But, sir," he said, "you don't seem to understand. I am not interested in one million dollars."

8

Dean Acheson
(1971)

On a fall evening, as the twilight came on, the control tower at Kennedy Airport stacked up some incoming jets to allow a flight of wild geese to go on their way unharmed to the south. As they passed over tidewater Maryland, an old man with a noble head and a bristling guardsman's mustache was sitting in his study on his Maryland farm. One minute he was a vigorous man, plagued however lately by a swollen eyeball. The next moment he slumped over, and at nightfall the news went out from Washington that Dean Acheson, President Truman's champion, friend, and field marshal, was dead. A thousand miles away, Mrs. Truman got the word and said she would not give it just then to the old president, who was frail and pretty much over the hill. But she guessed that he would be "very disturbed."

For once, it is possible to avoid a cliché with conviction. Acheson's going does not mark the end of an era. The era he dominated ended long before he died, and it took much fortitude and some humor to live serenely through the years when everything he had stood for was condemned or ridiculed or turned upside down, and when the European policy of the Truman administration was put down by a young generation of historians and columnists as a calculated effort to police the world and so bring on all our present woes. It is never possible, either when you're looking back on history or living it, to say for sure that B happened on account of A, simply because B followed A. *Post hoc, propter hoc* was called, by the old Romans, the grossest error of elementary logic. Unfortunately, it is one of the axioms that most of us live by. Nobody knows this better than politicians, and while they dread having it used against them, they leap to the chance to use it against the opposition. Next year, a presidential year, we shall certainly be hearing again from the Republicans that they are and always have been the true "party of peace." Because, when America went into the First World War and the Second World War, and into Korea, and into Vietnam—there was a Democrat in the White House. Ergo, the Democrats are the war party.

Dean Acheson was alive and well while a new generation was becoming articulate—verbose, anyway—and looking back in anger to the Truman-Acheson years. I cannot forget the first time I felt the blast of this new indignation. It was the late 1960s and I was up in Minnesota during its perishing winter, dashing out of twelve below zero into the ninety-degree oven of a university auditorium. I was to talk to an audience of a thousand or more students. They were polite and even cordial until I started to recall the years just after the Second World War, the threadbare years when Europe was an invalid and a total dependent of the United States, an invalid greatly alarmed by the Soviets' pressure first in northern Iran, then down in the Mediterranean, then during one terrifying summer in Berlin. I was not proposing a thesis, or even thinking to defend such blessings as we had come to take for granted: the Marshall Plan or the North Atlantic Treaty Organization.

What I was appalled to discover was that the great majority of these students had apparently never heard of the Marshall Plan. There was, however, a minority that knew of it and were pretty cynical about it, as about the first grand installment of an American insurance scheme: I realized, a little late, that when the Russians had been huffing and puffing, when all these great and awful things were happening, these students were unborn, and therefore Azerbaijan and the siege of Berlin and the Marshall Plan lay, for them, in that dead zone that exists in every mind between what is too late to get into the books and what is too early for you to have lived through. From hot little speeches masquerading as questions, I learned two separate and opposing prejudices about Truman and Acheson. One, they were sleeping partners of the late Senator Joseph McCarthy, quick to see Communism under every bed and reacting in panic with billions for arms. This opinion came, obviously, from students inclining visibly to the left. The other complaint came from the fewer leaners to the right: that on the contrary, both the president and his secretary of state were shameless "coddlers" of Communists.

This charge sprang from the disdain that both men expressed for loyalty oaths, and for McCarthy's trembling as-
sertions that there were scores of Communists on active
undercover service inside the State Department. In the presidential election year of 1952, the Republicans found this
propaganda line too tempting to resist and, mostly actively,
one Richard M. Nixon pictured Acheson as something very
close to a traitor if not an underground Communist agent.
There was a shabby scene at the Republican Convention in
1952 when somebody unfurled a banner inscribed with the
legend: "Acheson—Twenty Years of Treason" and there was a
thunderclap of cheers.

It would have been easy, it would have been forgivable self-
protection, for Acheson to throw a few sacrificial lambs in
the State Department to McCarthy's slaughterhouse. But he
never did. And when a minor official, one Alger Hiss, was
found guilty of passing on secret papers to the Soviet Union,
Acheson was on the touchiest ground of his public life. He
had been a friend of Hiss, and at his next press conference
he was asked how he felt about Hiss now. The secretary
had anticipated the question. He picked up the New Testament and said, "You will find the answer in the gospel according to St. Matthew." Pressed to say that Hiss was well
worth renouncing, he simply said, "I will not turn my back on
Alger Hiss." To the people who, like Acheson, probably
thought Hiss innocent, this was a courageous act of friendship; to the rest, to the Republicans especially, it was a typical
flourish of Acheson arrogance. In any case, it let off another
national uproar. *[It would take more than forty years for us to have*

access to the KGB and the Hungarian Communist archives, which revealed—what Acheson didn't know, nor for that matter did Mc-Carthy—that there really was at that time a small group of dedicated Communists in the State Department.]

During his last two years as secretary of state, Acheson's public appearances were frequently booed, he went in danger of physical harm, his telephone rang incessantly with threats and obscenities. I wondered at the time if he could survive all this without a breakdown. Somehow, under a strain his intimates agonized over, he managed. It is part of the common tragedy of the passing of time that those who know what such a man as Acheson did don't need to be reminded of it, and the rest are either too bored or too skeptical to care. Nevertheless, we had better remind ourselves that whether or not our present troubles stem from Truman and Acheson or from earlier or later times, Acheson was the man who, with one other man in the State Department, brought forth the Marshall Plan. Will Clayton conceived it, and Acheson delivered it.

Will Clayton's is a name you will not find in the almanacs or encyclopedias, though he came to play a great role backstage, away from the limelight, the great names, the powerful egos. A mild-spoken southerner, a businessman who had gone into diplomacy because he felt politicians were, on the whole, either ignorant of or indifferent to economics. He was not so much interested in how the war was to be won as how Europe was to renovate its shattered economy. Would it again manage a favorable balance of payments? Could there ever again in Europe be a prosperous commodity market?

These are not concerns that inflame the multitude. Clayton was sent by President Truman to Britain and to the continent of Europe to look over the devastation. Behind the ruined cities he saw, to his consternation, a general lack of the simplest goods of everyday life. He came back and at once devised a grand plan to restore the economy of Europe by direct aid from America, not the promise of aid later on, but grants, loans, massive American investment in steel, coal, mining, construction—Now! He wrote many memoranda on this big theme, enlisted the intellect and enthusiasm of Dean Acheson, General Marshall's second-in-command at the State Department, and brought in several economists, and the department's Soviet expert, George Kennan.

Together, they put together a speech, which Acheson proposed to give at a small college in Mississippi as a trial balloon for, perhaps, a presidential address later on. Acheson went down to Mississippi flushed with the belief that he was proposing nothing less than a plan "to restore the fabric of European life." Nobody paid attention, and a disheartened Acheson at once got hold of Clayton and made the audacious proposal that General Marshall, who was due to make the commencement address at Harvard, should substitute the body of Acheson's speech for whatever else he had meant to say. The general agreed, and Harvard had the honor of hearing the first presentation of the grand plan. But General Marshall's speaking style was so monotonous, his prose so flat: he was simply too thoroughly decent a man to have a spark of theater, a hint of ham, about him. Again, nobody—including the best newspapers—paid more than polite attention. Moreover, the promise of radical aid to European industries was deliberately vague, for Marshall knew that the temper of the Congress just then was to restrict American help to military aid for countries, like Greece and Turkey, that were palpably threatened by the Communists from within or without.

However, as I have told elsewhere, Ernest Bevin, the British foreign secretary, saw that the plan was nothing less than a massive attempt to rescue Europe from "hunger, poverty, desperation and chaos."

Two big problems stood like roadblocks in the way of moving the plan off the drawing board into action. Was the plan to include the Soviet Union, the newfound enemy, which had, like Britain, been a principal beneficiary of the lend-leasing of war materials? The answer was—yes. But would an American Congress pour out money for a former ally which was now giving every sign of meaning to overrun Europe? Luckily, for the other beneficiaries (and the passage of the plan!), the Soviets were against any beneficence to the whole of Europe. They would decide, one at a time, which nations qualified for aid. It was an impossible bid for precedence, and Molotov walked out in a huff proclaiming that the whole plan was an imperialist racket to swamp Europe with American goods and arms.

The next, and high hurdle, was Congress. Mocked and pilloried by Truman as a "Do Nothing" Congress, its Republican majority was not about to do his bidding. It was embittered by the tendency of the new European governments to turn left and was inclined to revert to its old isolationism, to leave "old sick Europe" to its own devices. This grudge was hardened by the well-publicized derision of the United States even by its most loyal recent allies. Bevin, the very foreign secretary who had "grabbed (the Marshall Plan) with both hands" had recently called Britain "the last bastion of social democracy . . . against the red tooth-and-claw of American capitalism and the Communist dictatorship of Soviet Russia." So now he was begging alms from the red tooth-and-claw!

At the time, it appeared to be an impossible sell to Congress. Marshall himself appeared before the Senate's Foreign Relations Committee and presented his case in his usual grave monotone. He was followed by Acheson. First, he suggested the folly of a piecemeal approach to this country and that toward which the Soviet Union had obviously malign intentions. He described more graphically than anyone else had done the ruination that Clayton had seen: the hundreds of miles of twisted railroad tracks, the bombed-out factories and shipyards, the rubble heaps of what once were city centers, the charred skeleton of a whole city that was Berlin. He glossed over the creative, more abstract, economic side of the plan and saved his passion for the theme that alone could swing the Senate to approve an appropriation of anything like the thirteen billion dollars that would eventually be disbursed.

He worked himself up to his main argument by recalling the swift brutality with which the Soviets had imposed Communist governments on Poland, Rumania, Hungary, Czechoslovakia, and warned it was not beyond belief that, unaided

90

and left to rebuild itself, the whole of Europe, a broken continent, poor and hungry—would be raw meat for the Soviet glutton. Seeing him glaring at the committee, his face as purple as a lobster in anger, I marveled then at the passion he managed to manufacture over this hellish prospect. Manufactured or not, his passion won the day. His throbbing testimony had given frightening reality to that Iron Curtain which, only a year before, Churchill had envisioned as the new and threatening division of Europe. "These people," Acheson pleaded, "are desperate. Simply to restore the fabric of European life, this thing must be done."

It was done. And in the long run, the children or the grandchildren of Acheson's present detractors will know who was the American who did it. More than most presidents, and public magnificoes, he deserves, somewhere in Europe, a statue. Make it an equestrian statue, with his cape rising in the wind from the east, and his mustachios bristling, and the inscription underneath: "Dean Gooderham Acheson, 1893–1971: To Restore the Fabric of Europe."

9

Eisenhower at Gettysburg

(1967)

Although as a working correspondent I had "covered" Eisenhower from the convention that nominated him on through his years as president, an invitation to go to Gettysburg and spend some days talking with the general about Churchill was one I accepted with alacrity. During several years of moonlighting as a television master of ceremonies, I had discovered that few casual experiences in peacetime offer such a rewarding and sustained glimpse of a man as that of working alone with him on a long television dialogue.

Intelligent actors complain that the chronic ordeal of their profession is "the waiting, not the acting." But it is during the waiting intervals, which tend to be prolonged and uncertain, that you can sit down and talk usefully with a man to no set purpose. And during the three days at Gettysburg, I spent many hours alone with the general (as he preferred to be called) talking in his office, and up at the farm, about everything from politics to golf, from the code of a soldier to the temptations of a newspaperman, from the private trials of the presidency to the public life of a small Kansas town in the early 1900s. We deliberately avoided elaborating on his reminiscences of Churchill, thinking it better to let these come out instinctively in the freewheeling talk that was done under the cameras.

The general was always cordial and relaxed in the mornings and again at the end of day. In between, he was inclined to fret at the unsoldierly routine of waiting for action that was unscheduled and unpredictable, and very often he would glance at his watch and screw up his eyes—as he always did when in doubt or suspicion—and wonder "what those fellows are up to." Inevitably, I suppose, a lifelong officer is put at his ease by knowing precisely what his subordinates are doing and when they are expected to appear at the double. He could never understand why a change of lighting or camera setup could take ten minutes or an hour, and to my assurances that everything was under control he would shake his head and concede that "it's a weird business." Then I would ask him about his favorite part of England, or what was the toughest course he had ever played, and he would light up again and be off in his earnest, restless, rollicking manner.

In the late afternoons, he retired to his house for a nap and soon afterwards appeared, amiable again. It was here that you could get a sharp impression of him in the years of his retirement. And it was here too that I found myself bringing into focus my own tentative judgment about his virtues in war and in peace.

By the time of this, our last, meeting, he was very much an old country squire, sitting on his terrace with his back to the light and the book held high in his hands because like many old men whose eyesight does alarming things from month to month, he was just then in between prescriptions, so to speak. So his glasses were perched on the end of his nose, and by holding the book high and looking through the bottom of the lenses he could get things in focus until the new bifocals arrived. From time to time he put the book down and squinted out across his fields to the pasture. And he would watch the cattle going in, or scrutinize a blighted elm, or re-mark that a particular feed grass he was using burned out too quickly in the drenching summer heat of that very hot valley.

We all, they say, revert to our origins in old age, and if you'd not known who Ike was you would have guessed, and rightly, that he was a lifelong farmer—and by now a prosper-ous one. They were having a fierce drought that summer in Pennsylvania, as everywhere else in the East, and as the sun declined and the evening became bearable, we strolled out onto the grass and towards a small circular lawn that was a precious thing to Ike. It was a rudimentary putting green and it had only one hole, with a flag stuck in it whose pennant was stamped with the five stars of a General of the Army. But, strangely, this hole was invisible; it was so grown over with weeds that I doubt you could have sunk a small cannonball in it. I asked about this and he said, in that hesitant yet stren-uous tone he brought to all questions of conscience: "Well, you see, the governor of Pennsylvania put out a proclama-tion over a month ago, I guess, asking people to save water and do no watering of lawns, gardens, golf courses and so on. Looks pretty sad, doesn't it?"

In retrospect, it was altogether a sad occasion. In his old age, there were two things Ike lived for: his farm and his golf. And the greater of these was his golf. At that time he was beginning to be plagued by innumerable ailments, and I remember on that particular day he was a little querulous because he had had some tests made on an affliction of his diaphragm, and the results were not in. But what worried him most was the arthritis in his hands. The next day he kept rubbing the joints and wondering if he would ever play golf again. I hinted, in a subsequent conversation, that he had the golf bug pretty badly. "In the worst way," he said. "I didn't really take it up until after the war when I was in my midfifties, when I was at SHAPE. And, as you know, it takes about two years to learn to hit the ball. And sometimes during briefing sessions, I'd let my mind wander from the disposition of the Russian armies and our NATO equipment and so on, and just worry about my game. There was a time when I used to dash out of Paris to St. Cloud and, by golly, I'd say never mind the Russian threat to Europe, if only I can straighten out this terrible duck-hook that I've developed."

If it happened just like that, I'm sure that no one felt more guilt about it than Ike. For he had, at all times, an overwhelming sense of mission—whether you agreed or not with the mission didn't matter. While he was in Paris, and while he was in the presidency, there were certain priorities in his mind that had the force of moral absolutes. One was the security of Western Europe, and we ought not to forget, in the ups and downs of European independence, that it was Ike's authority, and the certainty of the attitude he conveyed to the Russians, which kept Europe untouched in the dangerous days when the Soviet Union was sorely tempted to move into the southern periphery of Europe. It is a curious psychological fact, never satisfactorily explained, why the Russians seemed to respect the peaceful intentions of a professional soldier more than they did those of Ike's predecessor or his successors. Although American presidential election campaigns tend, by their ferocity and length, to cause the parties to overdramatize their differences and pretend they are offering the people drastically opposite policies, it may appear in time that American foreign policy, towards Europe anyway, was all of a piece from the day that President Truman warned the Russians about Greece to the day that President Johnson warned them again about Berlin. But the man who secured this policy and gave it stamina was Eisenhower. And for that, perhaps more than anything else, I believe, we are all in his debt.

Whether he was a great president, or even a very good one, is something that I don't think it possible to decide today. Arnold Toynbee, for example, has the rather alarming conviction that the man responsible for our present ills and the coming of Doomsday is Truman, and that John Foster Dulles's brinkmanship was only a way of saying what Truman had long ago been doing. Eisenhower, it seems to me, had two golden periods, of which the second was his first term as president. The first, of course, began with his appointment as Supreme Commander of the Allied Forces.

Many harsh things have been said about him as a soldier and about the "luck" of his promotion, over many superiors, to the American command in Europe. Among European commentators, Eisenhower's total inexperience as a field commander is by now almost a byword. From this literal fact the false inference is readily drawn that he was essentially a desk man quite out of touch with the demands of modern war. Nothing could be farther from the truth or, incidentally, reflect so poorly on General Marshall's judgment. Marshall had watched Eisenhower's masterly conduct of the vast Louisiana maneuvers in September 1941, a field exercise in a "war of supply" that few old field commanders had ever experienced.

It is true that Ike's most recent professional experience, that of creating a defense for the Philippines, brought him into immediate close contact with Marshall in the days after Pearl Harbor when the Philippines were the most vulnerable of America's outposts in the Pacific. But a desk man would have been routinely consulted and dismissed. Marshall threw at Ike the whole strategical problem of the Pacific, and Ike's quick decision that Australia must become the essential base to build and hold for the protection of China, the Philippines, and the Dutch East Indies coincided with Marshall's private, and unexpressed, judgment. Moreover, Marshall had at his elbow innumerable Eisenhower reports on what the shape of a two-ocean war might be. For, during his years as confidential adviser to the Army Chief of Staff, Eisenhower had become absorbed by the probable scope and character of a future global war: by "such subjects as the mobilization and composition of armies, the role of air forces and navies in war, tending toward mechanization, and the acute dependence of all elements of military life upon the industrial capacity of the nation. This last was to me of special importance because of my intense belief that large-scale motorization and mechanization and the development of air forces in unprecedented strength would characterize successful military forces of the future."

The plodding quality of the prose—"such subjects as," "all elements of military life," "tending toward mechanization"—disguises the novelty of a strategical doctrine that was revolutionary, at the least highly questionable, to the high command of both the British and French in the mid-1930s. An obscure French major, one Charles de Gaulle, had written by then an obscure little book, which had a pitifully small sale. It was called *The War of Movement.* It predicted the end of the traditional war of deep fortifications and prepared defensive positions. The Maginot Line, he suggested, was already obsolete. The new war would be one of rapid movement by highly mechanized forces, hundreds of tanks and murderous accompanying aircraft. (The only famous commander who was known to have been impressed by de Gaulle's book, and by two earlier, equally fantastical, German monographs, was Adolf Hitler. He rendered the Maginot Line obsolete by going round it, and he proved how successfully he "tended toward mechanization" by inventing the Blitzkrieg and devastating Poland within a week.)

Once the revolutionary nature of Eisenhower's thesis is recognized, it is not hard to see why General Marshall, having succeeded in resisting Roosevelt's persistent pleas to take the Supreme Command in Europe, had no other candidate in mind than the man who had started his career in tank training, the obscure fifty-year-old (named in early press reports Lt. Col. D. D. Ersenbeing) who had brilliantly conducted that mock "war of movement" with four hundred thousand men in Louisiana only two months before Pearl Harbor.

Eisenhower may not have been, like Montgomery or Rommel, a soldier's soldier (which, for good or ill, means a practiced old warrior). But he was, for the war years, the ideal choice also for a human task which the Allies of the First World War, bristling with a long tradition of military chauvinism, so stubbornly and grievously evaded: that of uniting by one likable and fair-minded personality the warring elements of many nations, many diverse temperaments, and some very rum characters. So that, apart from Eisenhower's early perception of the industrial shape of modern war, he had one touch of genius that could probably not have been found in any other known Allied military commander. Very soon after his arrival in England, and his early meetings with Prime Minister Churchill and the combined Allied command, he devised for himself a code, at once compassionate but strict, which forbade the use of pejorative slurs on any nationality of the alliance: "Any time I heard a man condemning somebody and saying he was a British so-and-so or an American so-and-so or whatever, I pointed out there was an order." An American colonel apparently defended himself by saying that his opposite number had argued harshly: "I don't care how harshly you argued, you said he was a British so-and-so. Go home!" The man was sent back to America and his military career was as effectively tarnished as that of one of Ike's oldest friends, General George Patton, after he had slapped a wounded soldier in a hospital bed. *His* fate was worse than any journey home. He was relieved of his beloved command, and from then on did Eisenhower's bidding.

Eisenhower's touch of genius was nothing very dramatic or much admired by the military of any nation. It was to be a peacemaker among Americans, Englishmen, Frenchmen, Poles and others crackling with national pride and driven by personal ambition. It may be that such immortality as, in the long run, Eisenhower achieves will be guaranteed by two qualities that do not usually, in a worldly world, secure a man much more than the affection of his friends. By the force of these qualities, Eisenhower was able to make trusting friends of about two hundred and fifty million people fighting for their lives. They are candor and decency.

10

Harold Ross

(1951)

One evening toward the end of 1923, there appeared this item, in the daily column of a popular New York journalist who often wrote a parody of Pepys's diary: "And to H. Ross's, and we talked about the low state periodical comick literature is sunk into."

It was true enough. But nobody in America apparently was doing anything about it. There was the old *Life*, and there was *Judge*, two family magazines whose stock-in-trade was deaf old ladies, comic valentines, he-she jokes, and a dreadful series of contributed saloon gags called Krazy Kracks. Sophisticated New Yorkers might wince at this stuff, but the instinct to wince was merely satisfying proof of their own urbanity.

Yet there was one man who winced for a living. He was coeditor of *Judge*, and as he corrected its laughing copy every wince was a stab at his pride, his taste, and his patriotism. He would reach in his drawer and finger the pages of *Punch* and

Simplicissimus and sigh over the superiority of Europe. He quit his job and turned to improve American humor with the almost suicidal frenzy of a Strindberg hero. He was impossibly cast for this part. He wanted to found a sophisticated, ironic metropolitan weekly. He was a gawky outlander, a runaway from a small town high in the Rockies, an itinerant newspaperman who had bummed his way to San Francisco, a doughboy who had gone AWOL to run an American army magazine from Paris, a cantankerous, poker-crazy, all-swearing, all-drinking westerner—Huck Finn in a slept-in business suit and cracked yellow shoes. He was, however, the H. Ross of "F. P.'s" little item. He looked for a wealthy backer and found one in the socialite heir to a yeast fortune.

In February 1925 he put out a thin, unlikely-looking first-born. It combined *Punch*'s Charivari with *Judge*'s two-line jokes. It had some comic strips barely dignified as "panels." There were a few local advertisements, some caricatures of actors, and art notes by "Froid." Its only note of superiority was a derisive promise that it would not be edited for "the Old Lady in Dubuque." Ross called it *The New Yorker.*

From that start, it lost two thousand dollars a week. It took three years and the outpouring of seven hundred thousand unrequited dollars to turn the red ink into black. Today, we are told, it may be bought by almost anybody with several million dollars to spare.

In 1950, a book appeared to celebrate that twenty-fifth anniversary, a miracle of longevity nobody knowledgeable about journalism, least of all H. Ross, could have imagined in the early days of its penury and of H. Ross's groping all over town to find a writing style that would fit the model magazine he held in his imagination. He never did find it, which only proved something terrifying about Harold Ross that no contributors, early or late, ever guessed at when they first encountered this naive lunkhead. It was the totally unsuspected perfectionism of his mind and the unanswered question of where he got it from. He had quit high school and, with precious little education, wanted to be and became a newspaperman. He had read one whole book through and never pretended otherwise. What nobody anticipated before they turned in their copy was his probing, unsleeping, fussy, appallingly unforgiving intelligence. He kept on his desk what he called his two "bibles": Fowler's *Modern English Usage* and Mark Twain's devastating diagnosis of the flatulence and related prose disorders of Fenimore Cooper. But he by no means regarded Fowler as gospel—he liked his precision and wit but when Fowler moved over the line from clarity to pedantry, Ross moved in on him as brutally as he did on any and every contributor, except two writers whose styles most nearly approximated to the impossible ideal: E. B. White and James Thurber.

Ross's literary ignorance made him no respecter of persons, however eminent. A writer who quoted Tennyson's "Nature red in tooth and claw" was immediately corrected. Ross's amendment read "Nature red in claw and tooth" with a note to the effect that a bloodthirsty animal would grab its prey by the claws before lifting it onto the teeth.

By the time the magazine's final proofs were passed on to the printer, Ross had read every line, much of the copy two or three times over. Before that longed-for Tuesday twilight, every contributor to the current issue had received, with his galley proofs, a typed page of numbered notes. They could run to ten or fifteen comments, varying from an abrupt single word ("Bushwah!") to a brief note of advice ("Could trim here" and "too detailed") to exasperated comments on the writer's dumbness ("Outside of what? And sheriff who? Who's he?") or verbosity ("For God's sake, there's no point in enumerating all these subsidiaries.")

Also unaccounted for was his exquisitely neurotic feel for syntax, a gift or a tyranny passed on to his deputy and non-fiction editor, William Shawn, who shared a similar sensitivity. (A book review I wrote in which I noted that the young and rebellious Churchill "almost completely ignored the school's syllabus" evoked a pained marginal comment: "*The New Yorker* does not recognize degrees of completeness." Touché!)

For Ross, there was no such thing as an "established" writer. Whether you were famous or a first contributor, your piece was subjected to the same disinterested, ruthless scrutiny, and every piece was accepted or rejected on what Ross alone decided were its merits—a procedure that in the later years outraged some authors presumed by the rest of the world to be the most treasured of *The New Yorker*'s writers. John O'Hara and even James Thurber frequently went into apoplexy at this brutal treatment. Such was Ross's writhing perfectionism that none of the permanent staff could remember a time when he ever wrote the comment "good" or "what we want." The best he was ever known to concede was "in the direction of what we want." "Comes the revolution," said Dorothy Parker, "and it will be everybody against Ross."

Because Ross went on looking for gold ("what we want") among the unlikeliest prospectors, and because he took no eminent writer for granted, he came by the end of the magazine's first decade to be showered with the best American writing, both from the celebrated and the obscure. He had given transatlantic fame to a crop of former unknowns: Dorothy Parker, Ogden Nash, Robert Benchley, James Thurber, Frank Sullivan, and among the cartoonists Peter Arno, Charles Addams, Otto Soglow, Whitney Darrow, and George Price. Alva Johnston resurrected the odd, intimate character sketch from where John Aubrey had buried it over two centuries ago and called it a "profile." The best reporting talent of the newspapers had been combed to establish a department, "A Reporter at Large," glorified by such previously unseen blushers as James Mitchell and A. J. Liebling. Less celebrated than Ross's recruitment of writing talent was his remarkable feat in discovering and exposing a cornucopia of comic artists. By the end of its first decade, the magazine had a stable of cartoonists as expert and personally distinguishable as *Punch's* in England. Here again, Ross's hand performed ruthless but curative surgery. He blotted out *Punch's* explanatory captions, sometimes running to five lines: Father *(an army Colonel returned from India who has just heard of his son's engagement):* . . . Son *(who is apprehensive about his father's approval)* . . . etc., etc., etc. Ross preferred, or rather dictated, an unattributed single line in quotation marks. If there was any doubt who was being spoken to he would note in the margin of the proof: "Open this mouth wider" or "No point if *she's* talking. Make clear." Occasionally, as with a naked man holding his nose and drowning in a shower, Ross gave four reasons, having to do with door locks, drains and other sanitary conveniences, why it was impossible for a man to drown in a shower. He held the drawing back from publication for a month, even though it was by the star artist, Peter Arno. The farthest Ross was ever known to go by way of expressed admiration was an appreciative "Right!" to George Price's own comment on his series of the old lumpen couple in the rickety beach house, where every water pipe, television connection, wall plug and oven accessory was beautifully drawn in. "No plumber," said Price, "ever criticized my drawings."

In its twenty-sixth year, *The New Yorker* had become an American institution, confident, prosperous, unsinkable. Now it entered its dangerous age. Ross himself knew it. He complained that looking among the young for new ideas, new writing, he found them weaned and bred to write a pallid imitation of the *New Yorker* style. Some of us feared, a decade or more ago, that to escape that fate (an incurably pallid *New Yorker*), the magazine might consciously try to change its prose style, to stiffen its character. In 1938, there appeared a cover drawing that belonged to no artist we knew. It was, though, by the ribald Peter Arno. It was of a herd of bowed heads: the Nuremberg victims. It showed at a shocking glance how alien to the oncoming world of violence was *The New Yorker* we cherished. For Hitler was outraging urbanity everywhere, like a Dostoevsky lunatic let loose in a country club.

We were wrong. E. B. White had set the tone of the "Talk of the Town" comments, indeed of the magazine's persona, and he had developed a modern vernacular style as original and influential as any since Sir Richard Steele's. But suddenly, he applied it to the great and grave issues of the day. *The New Yorker* was led into battle by a man who wrote like an angel and now felt like a man. And, to the honor of the unlettered grouchy Ross himself, the effect of his fussy and exacting standards over fifteen years was to produce suddenly a small team of war correspondents as gifted and memorable as any who covered the Second World War. And, after the war, the magazine melded, without strain or affectation, its new seriousness and its old irony and grace. Unfortunately, Ross never lived to see how completely he had transformed the civil face of English-American journalism, more than any editor this century. He died suddenly, in December 1951, just as he was fearing the magazine was about to decline into a pale imitation of the original, a "sophisticated" magazine as the word is understood by the readers of what he called "those fancy readers" of the fashion magazines.

11

The Legend of Gary Cooper
(1961)

When the word got out that Gary Cooper (who died aged sixty) was mortally ill, a spontaneous process arose in high places not unlike the first moves to sanctify a remote peasant. The Queen of England dispatched a sympathetic cable. The president of the United States called him on the telephone. A cardinal ordered public prayers. Messages came to his house in Beverly Hills from the unlikeliest fans, from foreign ministers and retired soldiers who never knew him, and from Ernest Hemingway, his old Pygmalion, who had kept him in mind, through at least two novels, as the archetype of the Hemingway hero: the self-sufficient male animal, the best kind of hunter, the silent infantryman padding dutifully forward to perform the soldier's most poignant ritual in "the ultimate loneliness of contact."

It did not happen to Ronald Colman, or Clark Gable, or—heaven knows—John Barrymore. Why, we may well ask, should it have happened to Frank James Cooper, the rather untypical American type of the son of a Bedfordshire lawyer, a boy brought up in the Rockies among horses and cattle to be sure, but only as they compose the unavoidable backdrop of life in those parts; a schoolboy in Dunstable, England, a college boy in Iowa, a middling student, then a failing cartoonist, failed salesman, an "extra" in Hollywood who in time had his break and mooned in a lanky, handsome way through a score or more of "horse operas"? Well, his friends most certainly mourn the gentle, shambling "Coop," but what the world mourns is the death of Mr. Longfellow Deeds, who resisted and defeated the corruption of the big city; the snuffing out of the sheriff, in *High Noon,* heading back to duty along the railroad tracks with that precise mince of the cowboy's tread and that rancher's squint that sniffs mischief in a creosote bush, sees through suns, and is never fooled. What the world mourns is its lost innocence, or a favorite fantasy of it fleshed out in the most durable and heroic of American myths: that of the taut but merciful plainsman, who dispenses justice with a worried conscience, a single syllable, a blurred reflex action to the hip, and who must face death in the afternoon as regularly as the matador, but on Main Street and for no pay.

Mr. Deeds Goes to Town marks the first jelling of this fame, and *The Plainsman* the best delineation of the character that fixed his legend. These two films retrieved Cooper from a run of agreeable and handsome parts, some of them (in the Lubitsch films for instance) too chic and metropolitan for his own good. At the time of *Mr. Deeds,* an English critic wrote that "the conception of the wise underdog, the shrewd hick, is probably too western, too American in its fusion of irony and sentimentality, to travel far." He was as wrong as could be, for the film was a sensation in Poland, the Middle East, and other barbaric regions whose sense of what is elementary in human goodness is something we are just discovering, perhaps a little late.

It is easy to forget now, as always with artists who have matured a recognizable style, that for at least the first dozen years of his film career Gary Cooper was the lowbrow's comfort and the highbrow's butt. However, he lasted long enough, as all great talents do, to weather the four stages of the highbrow treatment: first, he was derided, then ignored, then accepted, then discovered. We had seen this happen many times before; and looking back, one is always shocked to recognize the people it has happened to. Today the intellectual would deny, for instance, that Katharine Hepburn was ever anything but a lovely if haggard exotic, with a personal style which might enchant some people and grate on others, but would insist she was at all times what we call a "serious" talent. This opinion was in fact a highly sophisticated second thought, one which took about a decade to ripen and squelch the memory of Dorothy Parker's little tribute to Miss Hepburn's first starring appearance on Broadway: "Miss Hepburn ran the gamut of human emotions from A to B."

Marilyn Monroe is a grosser example still. Universally accepted as a candy bar or cream puff, she presented a galling challenge to the intelligentsia when she married Arthur Miller, a very somber playwright and indubitably *un homme sérieux.* The question arose whether there had been serious miscalculation about a girly calendar that could marry a man who defied the House Un-American Committee. The doubt was decided in Miss Monroe's favor when she delivered pointed ripostes to dumb questions at a London press conference.

At least until the mid-1930s there was no debate about Gary Cooper because he presented no issue. He belonged to the reveries of the middle-class woman. He reminded grieving mothers of the upright son shot down on the Somme; devoted sisters of the brother sheep-ranching in Australia; the New York divorcée of the handsome ranch hand with whom she is so often tempted to contract a ruinous second marriage in the process of dissolving her first. To the moviegoer, Cooper was the matinee idol toughened and tanned, in the era of the outdoors, into something at once glamorous and primitive. He was notoriously known as the actor who couldn't act. Only the directors who handled him had daily proof of the theory that the irresistible "stars" are simply behaviorists who, by some nervous immunity to the basilisk glare and hiss of the camera, appear to be nobody but themselves. Very soon the box offices, from Tokyo to Carlisle, confirmed this theory in hard cash. Then the intellectuals sat up and took notice. Then the Cooper legend took over.

For the past quarter century, Cooper's worldwide image had grown so rounded, so heroically elongated rather, that only some very crass public behavior could have smudged it. There was none. After a short separation he was happily reunited with his only wife. He spoke out, during the McCarthy obscenity, with resounding pointlessness and flourished the banner of "Americanism" in a heated way. Most recently, there has been a low-pressure debate in progress in fan magazines and newspaper columns about whether his "yup-nope" approach was his own or a press agent's inspiration, like the malapropisms of Sam Goldwyn, another happy device for blinding mockers to the knowledge that they were losing their shirts. This was decided a week or two ago by the *New York Post,* which concluded after a series of exhaustive interviews with his friends that Cooper's inarticulateness was natural when he was in the presence of gabby strangers, that gabbiness was his natural bent with close friends. He could probably have transcended, or dimmed, bigger scandals or more public foolishness than he was capable of, because he was of the company of Chaplin, Groucho Marx, W. C. Fields, Bogart, Louis Jouvet, two or three others, give or take a personal favorite. He filled an empty niche in the world pantheon of essential gods. If no cowboy was ever like him, so much the worse for the cattle kingdom. He was Eisenhower's glowing, and glowingly false, picture of Wyatt Earp. He was one of Walt Whitman's troop of democratic knights, "bright eyed as hawks with their swarthy complexions and their broad-brimmed hats, with loose arms slightly raised and swinging as they ride." He represented every man's best secret image of himself: the honorable man slicing clean through the broiling world of morals and machines. He isolated and enlarged to six feet three an untainted strain of goodness in a very male specimen of the male of the species.

12

Robert Frost
(1973)

It was a splendid day in Vermont when they buried Robert Frost, the sky without a cloud, the light from the white landscape making every elm and barn as sharp as a blade, and the people crunching quietly through the deep snow and squinting in the enormous sun.

It is a harmless sentimental custom to bury men who have been supreme in some craft with a visible symbol of their mastery: one thinks of composers whose tombstone is inscribed with a lyre, and cricketers who were laid to rest with a floral wreath of a bat and a ball. Few men must have gone to their graves amid such an exhibition of the tools of their trade as Robert Frost did the other day. From the smallest object on the horizon, a clump of evergreens or a mountain-top, to the most domestic scenery that was close at hand—a maple tree, a country store, a spade—everything the mourners saw or passed among had been the subjects of his poems and the objects of his lifelong meditation. He was once called "an original ordinary man," but whether we ordinary men are ready or able to understand an original among us is another question. And I wonder how many Americans could have honestly agreed with President Kennedy that Frost had "bequeathed this nation a body of imperishable verse from which Americans will forever gain joy and understanding." Because if his poetry was as plain as its surface, it was very ordinary indeed. And if it was as deep and difficult as his best admirers said, the understanding audience for it must have been as small as it always is for great poetry.

However, President Kennedy had taken him up, and in the last year or two he became a sort of unofficial Poet Laureate more honored, I suspect, for his connection with the White House than for any spontaneous response of the American people to the body of his work. At any rate, when he died, either eighty-seven or eighty-eight years of age (no one is quite sure), his last days were full of honor, love, obedience, troops of friends, as his early days had been full of menial farm chores, odd jobs that never paid off, and easygoing obscurity.

He was born in San Francisco of a New Hampshire journalist and a Scottish mother. His father died when he was ten, and his mother took him back East to settle in Lawrence, Massachusetts, and he became and remained a New Englander. From his nineteenth year to his thirty-eighth he managed to get only fourteen poems in print. In the meantime, he had tried and failed to be a student at Dartmouth College, but he did later stick out two years at Harvard. In the five years between these two grim efforts to be formally educated he was a bobbin boy in the mills, a cobbler, a small-town editor, a schoolteacher, and at last a farmer. But the soil of New England, as he came to reflect later, is a glacial relic, for most of the year the victim of alternating fire and ice. For this reason, or possibly because he was too obsessed with the natural objects of the countryside to be a good farmer, he had to eke out a living; which he did by going from his chores to teach English at one country school and to try teaching "psychology" (a new fetish discovered by William James) at another.

So in his thirty-seventh year he was neither a prosperous farmer nor an accepted poet. From his long meditations on the country life and landscape of New England he had shored up two small books of poems: *A Boy's Will* and *North of Boston*. Neither of them found a publisher until he moved to England in 1912 with the set intention "to write and be poor without further scandal in the family." There he lived and walked in the West Country and was befriended and admired by Wilfrid Gibson and Edward Thomas, two early Georgians with whom he seemed at the time to have a lot in common. He had left America with a family reputation as a dilettante, but when he came back he was greeted, by a small audience, as a pro. He had no more trouble making a modest living, and for nearly thirty years, on and off, he lived on another farm, was the so-called poet in residence at Amherst, and did other agreeable stretches as a teacher at the University of Michigan, at Harvard, but mostly at Middlebury College in Vermont, and then again at Dartmouth. He put out his books of poetry at about five-year intervals until the 1940s saw him at the peak of his productivity and his authority, bustling around "collecting sticks"—as he used to put it—for what he would ignite as annual "poetic bonfires."

From 1924 on he took the Pulitzer Prize for poetry at regular—about six-year—intervals. This habit, because it set him up as a solid Establishment poet, made his more intellectual admirers begin to think that there must be less in his work than met the eye. Indeed, Frost suffered for a long time from the incapacity of the critics to overcome certain stock responses to various schools of poetry that were then in fashion. Because he had been a friend of the English Georgians, he was for too long taken by some people to be an oversimple rebel against the developing technology of modern life, an expatriate cricket-and-ale rustic. And because, when he got back to America, he met the high tide of the "new" poetry of the Chicago school, he had to be looked on as a New England Sandburg. And because, in the 1930s, he maintained his lifelong lack of interest in politics, the socially conscious writers of the New Deal dismissed him as a cranky escapist. We never seem to learn—though the evidence is stacked high in any library—that contemporary prejudices about a writer very rarely seem relevant in the long view. Frost was, in fact, as absorbed, and in some ways as difficult, a poet as Emily Dickinson, whose entire meditations on life were conducted inside the house in Amherst, Massachusetts, from which she barred all visitors and rarely stirred in more than twenty years. Frost was, let us say, an outdoor Emily Dickinson, which is a curiosity almost too bizarre to bear thinking about. Even when he was writing what later was admitted to be his finest poetry, his admirers were again of the wrong sort to satisfy the literary lawmakers. The people who called him "our classic New England poet" also tended to see Will Rogers as the Mark Twain of the 1920s, and Pearl Buck as the traveling George Eliot of the 1930s. This is a kind of reverse sentimentality and a usual reflex of highbrows, who are often more concerned to validate a man's reputation than to enjoy him. It never troubled Frost much, and it would be a mistake to think of him at any time as a martyr. But for many years it made good men back away from him.

Other people, who were willing to be impressed, were put off by more honest reasons. They turned with pleasurable anticipation to his work, and what did they find? They found verses as limp and bare, and frequently as limp with bathos, as the verses on a country calendar. But if you persisted with him, you found that he persisted ahead of you. Sometimes he reads like a man with no poetical gift whatsoever who is determined to slog his way through some simple fact of nature and discover, at all costs, some universal truth. But what ought to give pause to the unwary is that there *is* always a mind at work, a wriggling, probing, and in the end a tragic mind. The very titles of his poems are deceptively ordinary. "The Cow in Apple Time," about a cow drooling cider, sounds like a humdrum thing. But it is not. Listen.

> . . . Having tasted fruit,
> She scorns a pasture withering to the root.
> She runs from tree to tree where lie and sweeten
> The windfalls spiked with stubble and worm-eaten.

She leaves them bitten when she has to fly.
She bellows on a knoll against the sky.
Her udder shrivels and the milk goes dry.

It was not until after the Second War, when the flame of the Harriet Monroe revolution had died down, and left so many of its fiery figures mere cinders along the way, that another generation of critics noticed Frost still there, still writing his knotty monosyllables. They began to be excited by the suspicion that here possibly was an American Donne, or a Yankee Theocritus, or—a harder thing to grapple with—Robert Frost, an original. The idea that a huckleberry or a birch tree, or the games a boy played—with that birch tree—who was "too far from town to learn baseball"; the idea that these things could bear the most unsentimental and profound contemplation was at first frightening, until the reader inched his way through the roughness of the underbrush and, like "A Soldier"—in Frost's poem—discovered that

. . . the obstacle that checked
and tripped the body, shot the spirit on
Further than target ever showed or shone.

By the time that he was being accepted as a pure and gritty-minded pastoral poet, about as far removed from the Georgians as Thomas Hardy or Brer Rabbit, he himself was rejecting the physical world as a tremendous harbinger of winter and sickness. You could say more simply that he was a genuine poet and the oncoming of old age stirred him:

Petals I may have once pursued
Leaves are all my darker mood.

At the age of seventy he was ready to upbraid God for the fate of Job and for His general cruelty to the human race. This challenge, in "The Masque of Reason," was too much for him, but by now the critics were ready to grant that unlike any poet before or since, Frost had used the ordinary vernacular of a New England farmer to probe a few fundamental doubts. In poetry that is subtler in structure even than most vernacular, he transmuted rocks and flowers, wind and berries and hired men, and striking mill workers, and boys swinging on trees, into the purest symbols of what is most hardy but most perishable in the human condition.

To the great mass of Americans, I suppose, he was simply a noble old man, said to be a great poet, who had come to be a colorful human adjunct to the refurbishing of the White House, rather like one of those plain hooked rugs, woven by a grandmother, with which wealthy New Englanders or Virginians living in exquisite Colonial houses will sometimes pay a small tribute to their origins. He must have learned to live with the knowledge that to most of his countrymen he was known only by a couple of lines from one poem, "Stopping by Woods on a Snowy Evening," just as John Donne must groan in his grave at all the twentieth-century people who know him only by the thought that "No man is an island." In our time, which is the age of mass marketing, we have to package our great men as quickly and simply as possible to make them acceptable to the family trade.

At the end, though, there was a lucky occasion on which his true readers and his uncomprehending large public could see him alike for what he was. In the icicle brilliance of Kennedy's inauguration he stood in twelve degrees of frost and tried to read aloud a poem specifically written for the great occasion. The sun stabbed at his failing eyes, the wind slapped at him, the white light from the snow was too much for him, and he finally gave up and spoke out, stumblingly, what he knew, his fingers kneading his palms in a secret fury and his white hair blowing in sloppy waves against his fore-head. It was an embarrassing moment for the president and the officials who had brought him, and for the huge crowd. But it was as good an end as any he might have imagined: an old farmer stripped down at last to a blinded oak of a man, tangled in his own branches, made foolish by the sun and the cold and the wind, by the simple elements he had once re-joiced in but which now he had come to mistrust as the mockers of humankind from Eden to Washington, D.C.

13

Goldwater:
Jefferson in the Desert
(1998)

They call it, always called it since the white man came there, the Salt River Valley.

The trouble with the word "valley" for those of us who live in temperate climates is: it calls up a picture of a cozy plain lying between the hills. But what I have in mind is a semitropical stretch of pure desert, forty miles east and west, twenty north and south, a vast silent plain of yellow, brown land: what Balzac called "God, with Man left out." The only upright things that interrupt the forty-mile flats are saguaro cactus trees, which look like spiky giants with their arms upraised in the act of surrender. Here the cold month is January, getting down as low as fifty degrees Fahrenheit—in midsummer, it's mostly over a hundred degrees, in any discoverable shade. Here, for how many centuries nobody can truly guess, an Indian tribe built adobe houses, dug canals, prospered at farming and disappeared. The only name they are known by is unlikely to be their true name: Hohokam—meaning "the people who have gone."

Flash forward to the late 1860s. Bang in the middle of this desert a white man, a prospector, pitched a tent, saw there was water from the nearby Salt River, and old canals to run through. He set up a hay camp, then grew other crops. (Contrary to the popular city folks' belief, the desert is wonderfully fertile—they always say "Spit on the desert and a flower will grow.")

Within a year, along came a young man who would help the prospector build new canals and mount eight-mule teams to haul supplies forty miles to the nearest army camp. This pioneer was an Englishman with the improbable name of Darrel Duppa. As always in the West, an Englishman, on account of his fancy accent, was given a title. He was known in Arizona as "Lord" Darrel Duppa. He is described—in the only book I can find a mention of him—as "an adventurer, scholar, inebriate and all-around regular fella." He comes into the story here for one memorable reason. Once settled in this primitive village, he looked around at the prehistoric mounds and the ancient canals—thought of the once-prospering tribe and thought to call this place after the mythical bird that was consumed by fire but always rose from the ashes. "From this village," he said, "will arise a city, Phoenix-like from the ashes of the past." They called it Phoenix. It is so today, and it is the capital city of Arizona.

In no time, the village acquired the primitive necessities: adobe houses, a store or two, butcher shop, a rude hotel, half a dozen saloons and—though it didn't yet have paved streets, it manufactured ice and delivered it in wheelbarrows. And once the railroad came through, bearing new westbound Americans, many of them stayed and baited the natives who, by then (a few hundred) were mostly Mexicans. There was not much rejoicing in those days in the prospect of multiculturalism, and weekend brawls between newcomer Americans and the Mexicans, to the accompaniment of random gunfire, soon compelled the necessity of a courthouse and a jail.

There were 1,800 inhabitants when the place was incorporated as a city and, after a boisterous election, got itself a city council to replace a vigilante band that had handled the frequent murders with straightforward lynchings. Now Phoenix had a legal government and legislators, who loved to call themselves Solons. First thing a western town official did once he got elected (this is a detail that the movies have always got right) was to go off and buy himself a silk hat. In the desert? He repaired at once to the shop of a recently arrived Pole—a Jewish immigrant, name of Goldwasser. Mr. Goldwasser was—when he wagoned into Arizona—a traveling tailor. He traveled no more. He settled in Phoenix and eventually started a chain of clothing stores and, in time, Arizona's first department store: with a large painted sign proclaiming Mr. Goldwasser's new—English—name: Goldwater.

This tailor was the grandfather of Barry Goldwater, former United States senator from Arizona, once Republican candidate for president—a thoroughly defeated candidate who had more historic influence on his party's future than any other defeated presidential candidate you can name. Who now, except professional historians, remembers William

Crawford, Lewis Cass, Alton B. Parker, even Michael Dukakis?

But Barry Goldwater. The present senator from Arizona, who succeeded Goldwater when he resigned, said at the funeral on Wednesday: "In all the histories of American politics, Barry Goldwater will remain a chapter unto himself. The rest of us will have to make do as footnotes."

Barry Goldwater died last week in his ranch house overlooking the Salt River Valley. He was eighty-nine. And I have gone into the history of the place his grandfather came to, because it explains why Barry Goldwater was a new American type as a presidential candidate. He was a frontier westerner. It was as if John Wayne or Gary Cooper had come to take over a New York gents' club. Before him, the Republican party had drawn its presidential runners from the Eastern cities and the farming Midwest. The people who ran the party were upper- and middle-class Eastern Establishment.

For thirty years, the Democratic party had seen itself captured and overwhelmed by Franklin Roosevelt and his introduction of Lloyd George's (more accurately, Bismarck's) Welfare State, administered by a strong central government. The force of this policy on a depressed nation, and its eager acceptance by the voters, compelled successive Republican candidates to bemoan the New Deal but accept its methods and beg to be reelected so they could perform it better. It looked, for a time, as if the Republican party and its old beliefs would never rise again. Roosevelt's successor was a shrewd and boisterous midwestern disciple: Harry S. Truman. Then there was—in Goldwater's version—a lamentable blip: General Eisenhower, who had decided to be a Republican and ran as such. Goldwater called him "a dime store New Dealer."

Suddenly, at the Republican Convention in San Francisco in 1964, out of the desert sprang this straight-backed, immensely handsome Barry Goldwater. "Immensely" was carefully chosen—he looked like one of the presidential figures carved in rock on that western mountain.

At that convention, which spurned the Eastern Establishment and its leader, and nominated Goldwater, he shouted: "Extremism in the defense of liberty is no vice." I don't suppose many of the millions listening to it figured out what it meant, but it sounded manly and downright and the convention hall shook under the roaring applause. The word "extremism" was just what the Democrats wanted to hear.

The Democrats had only to remind the voters that Goldwater had backed the malodorous Senator McCarthy in finding Communists everywhere, and they had him whipped before the vote. Add, on election eve, the note that the senator had voted against the first Civil Rights act, which abolished the segregation of the races. In truth, Goldwater abhorred segregation, had long ago integrated the Arizona National Guard and many years before brought blacks into the running of his family department store. But Goldwater felt, and said, "It's not the government's part to make men moral. Integration should be left to the states." If they don't do it, he implied, they ought to be ashamed of themselves. It was a little too idealistic for most people, who knew that left to themselves many states would have stayed segregated forever.

In truth, Goldwater's flaw as a practicing politician of high principle was a streak of naïveté which allowed him to embrace as allies shabby people and malicious people who simply said aloud they were against the things he was against. He assumed they shared his principles when all they shared was a gross prejudice. Senator Joseph McCarthy, even the hysterical Birch Society, were acceptable as fellow warriors. ("They're against Communism, aren't they? Nothing wrong in that.") When sixty-seven senators voted to censure McCarthy and dismiss his career into oblivion, Goldwater did not join them. When the House Judiciary Committee voted articles of impeachment against President Nixon, Goldwater was crushed. He had trusted Nixon absolutely. But once he pondered the notorious tapes, and watched Nixon's subsequent writhings of self-justification, Goldwater was appalled. Nixon, he now discovered, "lied to the Congress, lied to the people, lied to his own men. He was the most dishonest individual I ever met in my life."

The fact is that Goldwater lived by a few amazing simplicities: self-reliance, work hard, do good, help your neighbor, shrink the government. He learned these things from the daily experience of frontier life and his father's stories. But his political principles came from a very odd source. At a rally I covered in a California valley he shouted: "I have always stood for government that is limited and balanced and against every concentration of government in Washington." That, like many other obstinate sentences that were loudly applauded, came from Thomas Jefferson—but by way of Goldwater's talks with his grandfather. That immigrant tailor—like most central European immigrants—was familiar with pogroms and dictatorial government. But he was also a nineteenth-century Pole whose hope for his life in America lay in the works of Thomas Jefferson.

The paradox here is that for generations, the Democrats had always felt of Jefferson as their own ideological property. But they fixed on his pronouncements about liberty and free speech and never on his central passion: that the best government is the least government.

After his defeat, and for the next quarter century, Goldwater stayed in the Senate till he was eighty. He was regarded by the Democrats as a harmless, charming man. To the conservative Republicans of the South and West whom he had helped to take over the party, he was a renegade, because he turned out to be in favor of abortion and approved homosexuals in the armed forces. He saw nothing inconsistent in this with his ideas that government should stay out of private life—out of religion (he loathed the Christian coalition evangelists). Abortion? "Something no *man* should tamper with." Homosexuals in the army: "It doesn't matter if you're straight—what you have to do is shoot straight."

At that huge rally in the California valley in 1964, I couldn't help noticing that the loudest cheerers were not Jeffersonian philosophers. His simple slogans—anti-big-government, anti-Communist, no compulsory civil rights—attracted to his cause crowds of old-boy rowdies and simple bigots. When the rally was over, I wrote what occurred to me then as the tragedy of his campaign: "The rally is over. The good-natured crowd disperses to its Cokes and televisions and plans to collect 'bucks for Barry.' The night closes in and leaves us still with the galling contradiction between the Goldwater character and the Goldwater mania. He has no strain of demagoguery in him. He detests racial discrimination, but the ingrate South listens and sees the Negro foiled. He thinks of Jefferson, and his audience looks on Caesar."

14

Chichester:
The Master Mariner
(1967)

Late in the hot afternoon of July 4, 1962, three of us hurried off to Staten Island, went aboard a small yacht built like a miniature destroyer, which is to say like a carving knife, and pitched and rolled out to sea to look for Chichester. He was about to beat his own record for a single-handed crossing of the Atlantic, and he had been sighted vaguely south-southeast of Long Island. We figured he would round Ambrose Light long before dark, and we hoped so because the Lower Bay was cluttered with every sort of holiday boat as well as the normal heavy traffic, and slicing in through all those carefree patriots by night would be a tricky business.

The sun went over and was soon a pink haze behind us. The silver water turned to lead and we got out into heavy swells and felt queasy on more counts than one. Soon the lights went on at Rockaway Point and then we were abreast of the Light and the horizon was a pencil across an empty sky.

There were possibly twenty minutes or so left of our short twilight in which we could hope to see *Gypsy Moth III*, and be seen by her one-man crew.

Suddenly a sail moved up over the sea with the mechanical motion of a cardboard target in a shooting alley. It was a tiny ship, a ridiculous forty-odd-footer, but it ballooned over the horizon like Turner's *Fighting Téméraire* and through the glasses we saw its astounding captain, a small compact frame standing amidships, a peaked cap surmounting sideburns, thick glasses and the face of an aging lobster. Two hours later, when we had wriggled through all the nighttime horrors we had feared and were tied up at Staten Island, we drank a toast with him and saw him closer still, this iron little man who is imperturbable almost to the point of listlessness and looks like one of those carved wooden figures they sell in Broadway novelty stores or the papier mâché comics that rock outside the House of Nonsense at Coney Island. A very rum sort of hero, Popeye in the flesh.

Aside from the customs man there were only his wife and two others of us to greet him, and none of us dreamed that five years later a hundred thousand people would sit beside the flares on the ramparts of Plymouth Hoe, and a little after that the new Sir Francis would stand in the Quadrangle of the Royal Naval College at Greenwich while Elizabeth the Second repeated the ceremony of more than three and a half centuries ago and tapped him on the shoulder with the sword of Francis Drake. But sitting amid the ropes and bottles, sextants, sardine tins and all the mess of his little cockpit, he had done what he promised himself that night as he clocked his record time rounding Ambrose Light. To us he mentioned it casually as "the big trip." To the reader of this petrifying and heroic journal* he records the vow more gravely. "After (that) solo voyage across the Atlantic, I decided there was a chance of circumnavigating the world solo in an interesting and attractive way." This must be the blankest understatement since Lord Melbourne, having just seen Othello strangle Desdemona, remarked, "How different from the private life of our own dear Queen."

All the world now knows the plot of Chichester's mighty voyage: 29,630 miles alone, often in atrocious seas, one of the three small boats of eight to make it round the Horn; the longest passage ever made by a small sailing vessel—15,517 miles, from Sydney to Plymouth—without a port of call; twice as long as any passage ever made by a single-hander; the fastest voyage around the world—almost twice as fast as the previous best; only the third true circumnavigation round the Horn by a small ship where the track passed over two points antipodean to each other. The other records are listed (not by Chichester) in an epilogue. For him, there were two ambitions: to show that at sixty-five he had the reserves of character—of patience, ingenuity, intelligence and fortitude—to do it; and to do it with speed as a proof of good seamanship. And here, at last, is the journal of the whole adventure.

I have lately read two biographies by what you might call physical heroes, one of them a renowned flyer. They were so

*Gypsy Moth Circles the World, *by Sir Francis Chichester.*

full of conceit and pretension, and the dreadful awareness of an audience looking on saying "Is he the hero we think he is?" that they are drained of all humanity. The genius of Chichester is his total unselfconsciousness. The detestable word "image" has escaped him. He is absorbed with whatever is absorbing him at the moment: whether to go below (in a Force 11 wind!) and rescue the gear lever throttle control from the incoming flood, whether to reject the Admiralty directions for square-riggers to pass southeast of the Horn (he went north in his battered ship in order to stay upright), whether baked beans would be better for him than gin and lemon. This naive absorption with whatever was happening— the failing self-steering mechanism or the ghastly smell of his cases of eggs—guarantees the reader the pleasure of a man talking to himself without any suspicion that the stuff is going into print or between hard covers or—so help us—into a Book of the Month selection. His style is as bald and majestic as Defoe describing in a few syllables some awful detail of the Plague Year. He has the wonderfully engaging simpleness and irritability (with himself) of Pepys, and in his humdrum acceptance of illness and misfortune he recalls some of the journals of the Forty-Niners. The man is, no question, an heroic throwback. At various times he has a bad leg, a raging toothache, blinding headaches, various cuts and pustules, depression and—a few hundred miles from Sydney—total exhaustion and delusions. All the while he is thanking God for the smallest mercies and checking his daily list of things to do—"fix tarred twine for anti-chafe tie backs, repair bolt of the sheave in the fife rail, examine crosstree leads at deck and fuse, dry out bag of winter woollies, sow wheat germ." They amount to never less than seventy-five tedious duties a day, on top of the backbreaking chores of a one-man crew that rarely leave him more than an hour or two to sleep or eat. Round the Horn, with sixty- or eighty-foot waves yawning after him, he thinks, "Christ! What might it be like in a 120-knot wind?" and understands why the clipper ship captains told their men never to look astern. It took him two weeks to clean up the ruin from his capsizing, but he always wants to know why; from the fragment of a broken bottle, he is able to deduce that "the boat had turned through 131 when the bottle flew out of its niche; in other words, the mast would have been 41 below the horizontal."

It makes *Twenty Years before the Mast* sound like an America's Cup log. To yachtsmen, it will be as invaluable as Izaak Walton to fly fishermen, as Blackstone to lawyers. To the ordinary reader it is nothing less than the record, told in fine masculine English devoid of eccentricity or jargon, of a sustained ordeal probably unique in human history. An astounding and noble book.

15

Reagan:
The Common Man Writ Large
(1967)

The road to Ronald Reagan goes northeast across San Francisco Bay, up through the postwar industrial litter of the San Pablo shore, over the brown foothills of the Coast Range, out across the broad farmlands of the Sacramento Valley, and along by the Sacramento River to its confluence with the American River, where Sutter's boss carpenter, James Marshall, sat down on a January day in 1848 and examined some little yellow particles that had flaked through the tailrace of Sutter's sawmill. They were gold.

It is an appropriate introduction to the hero of *Death Valley Days*, the decent young pioneer of many a B Western who now finds himself the governor of California, the first choice of California, the first choice of Republican county chairmen, and the second choice of Republican voters for the presidency.

You are taken to him through corridors of exhibits extolling the bounty of the California counties, and then through a cabinet room newly done over by Mrs. Reagan as a handsome museum of Californiana with early Spanish furniture, watercolors, Indian prints, Argonaut memoirs. Beyond this bastion of nostalgia and flanked by the American flag on one side and the flag of the Golden State on the other, sits in his small study the fifty-six-year-old governor, a slim dark-haired man with the figure of a ranch hand, a college boy's grin, and an engaging manner quite his own. If you are a liberal or New Leftist spy expecting Everett Dirksen's senatorial piety, you are in for a disappointment. Equally, if you are a Birchite or other dinosaur hoping for the patriotic bellow and the double-armed all-American embrace, the man is a letdown.

Contrary to the campus rebel's view of him as an executive smoothie, there is no gloss to his rather craggy complexion, no whiff of pine needle aftershave lotion. His clothes do not give off the static electric charge of Madison Avenue vice presidents grounded on ankle-deep carpets. He looks rather like a peregrinating secretary of a large union whose blue shirt and dapper suit have spent many a day squashed in the hold of a jet plane. He could be a *Guardian* correspondent!

This first impression is well taken, since for many years he was the president of SAG (the Screen Actors' Guild) and traveled the country on the chicken, pea and mashed-potato circuit organizing and contracting for thirty-one affiliate unions of the American Federation of Labor. There was a lot of wrangling and all-night negotiations and general bitchery and betrayal there, enough experience of the political grind, anyway, to discredit the rather tedious ribaldry about a B-film actor turned governor.

The truth is that an actor is a laborer, too, and in the Depression, through the war, and afterward, he bowed to what the studios decided was his worthy hire. So Reagan was "Ronnie," the crackling young New Dealer, resisting goon squads, fighting the industry for livable contracts, an Americans for Democratic Action man, and later the keen helper of Helen Gahagan Douglas, the liberals' goddess, in her campaigns for Congress.

How come, you feel compelled to ask him, that an ADA liberal, a big Roosevelt man, and union organizer on the Clifford Odets model, turned Republican, and what's more a conservative Republican? Was there, over a time, some well-remembered trauma perhaps that profoundly changed his views? He knotted and unknotted his knuckles.

"Well, after the war there was a motion picture jurisdictional dispute between two unions. As president of SAG, I asked both unions to sit down with us. We met for seven months, twice a day, we had our own Panmunjom, and once you thought you'd got an equitable settlement, one side would come in with seventeen new lawyers and seventeen new deals. You couldn't believe it, then friends of mine would say, 'Come on, Ronnie, don't be so naive, we're simply following orders. You want us to show you the card?' I didn't even believe then there were such things as Communists, but they had the whole deal tied up. If we dug in, pickets were provided, homes were wrecked, and so on.

"Once I went to Washington on behalf of thirty-odd unions

to expound our tax policy to the House Ways and Means Committee. When I got there I was handed a booklet—'This is the AF of L's tax policy, this is what you read.' Of course, it had the government's support. When I got home I said to my wife: the tone of the speech is going to have to change, it's happening to other people. I'd been against trading our individual rights away to the industry. There came a time when I wasn't going to trade my rights away to the government."

His old friends mentioned, too, his shocked discovery that once you decide to build a home, you can suffer union slow-downs, inflated contracts, featherbedding, and somehow fail to own the house you've saved for without an albatross of a mortgage. Of course, there is no Republican, as there is no Catholic, like a convert. He reacted all right, but he reacted back to Jefferson, reading him in his own context and not in the chosen bits the New Dealers used for special purposes. It explains, I think, his strong tie to Goldwater, who remains a fervent Jeffersonian, the twentieth century notwithstanding. Unfortunately, the twentieth century has been unloosed on Reagan in the shape of an avalanche, which is to say the modern California that spawns and compounds all the technological vitality and the social ills that will one day afflict us all.

So, for over a year now, he has been sitting in Sacramento, under the great white dome of the State Capitol, and, in the contrived intervals of a working schedule as tight as an invasion plan, he is off and around the country at rallies, college debates, and banquets, raising packets for the Republican campaign fund, a service that is done in an orgy of altruism or on the off chance, about which he is not quite able to convey the incredulity he mimics, that he might hold the trumping ace over the next Republican Convention, and panic it into nominating him for president.

For the time being, there's no doubt that he has his homegrown troubles. His handling of them is more significant than it would be in Vermont or, for that matter, in Ohio, because in twenty-five years California has developed from a lush fruit bowl, film studio, and sunny haven for retired farmers and playboys into the first state of the Union in more things than numbers. All the chronic social, industrial, and rural problems of America today are here in acute form. A man who can administer California with imagination and good order is one who, unlike anyone else, except perhaps a mayor of New York City, would hold powerful credentials to preside over the United States.

Once you have boasted about the power, the population, and the resources of the first state of the Union, you have to do something about the jungle growth of the cities; the turmoil on the campuses; the conflict about compulsory unionism between organized labor and the freewheeling labor force; the unceasing inflow of 1,200 new settlers a day, loading the relief rolls and straining the welfare budget; not to mention the bewildering mobility of hundreds of thousands of part-time workers, deadbeats, runaway hippies, "suitcase" farmers, and the shuttling agents of the Mafia.

All this is producing ruinous invasions of the treasury and subjecting a governor who campaigned on economy to the embarrassment of a record five-billion-dollar budget, which by state law he is bound to balance. "In the last eight years," he says, "the budget has had a twelve percent annual increase. Last year it was sixteen percent." He puts this down partly, of course, to the openhanded fiscal extravagance of his predecessor, the Democrat "Pat" Brown. But after a few months of a new administration the voters are indifferent to the sins of the absent: they ask the immemorial question of the incumbent, "What are you doing for me right now?"

Committed to a show of economy, he maintains that inflation and the state's growth would justify an annual budget increase of just over seven percent. He has doggedly instituted a study of the tax system to try to achieve this miracle. But the demands of welfare, Medi-Cal, and free higher education for everybody "are increasing at a rate so fantastic that to satisfy them we'd have to have a state tax increase every two years. Illinois, for instance, has reduced the number of people on welfare by eight percent. Ours goes up by fifty-four point six percent a year! And Medi-Cal by something between thirty and sixty percent." Medi-Cal is California's name for the state medical care program which the federal Medicare law allows each state to adopt. Reagan believes that in this, as in other forms of bounty, the theory of social welfare has gone way beyond the capacity of the state to afford.

"Look at this," he snaps as he slides open a drawer and seizes a handbill, a promotion item for a free state convalescent hospital: "fully carpeted rooms, modern automated beds, the best of modern treatment, television, three succulent entrees on every menu; the atmosphere of a resort hotel." This, he says, "is a delusion—that you can give everybody free the same level of care as the richest man can afford. The medically indigent are something else—and they should come first. But we've given a credit card to one million three hundred thousand people."

In his big hassle with the regents of the University of California about "the traditional right of free education," he tried, and failed, to institute a small tuition fee. He believes that somebody, the federal government or the state, is going to have to charge a fifty-cent fee for a doctor's visit, something for drugs, and some check on the general assumption "that you can dash off to a brain surgeon with a headache." "I think you will find," he says without producing the documents, "that in the countries where they've introduced a national health service, they have underestimated their health budget by as much as five times." California, at any rate, seems to be having its own grim experience of subsidizing hypochondria on a mammoth scale.

What about the cities? He heaves a sigh and pops a cough drop in his mouth against what he grinningly describes as "a slight case of instant pneumonia." He has deep doubts about the President's Commission study, or about encouraging the surplus farm population to come into the cities. "My God, the OEE [Office of Emergency Employment] brought the Indians in. It was a disaster—they learned to be delinquent, or alcoholic. I think we have to take a new look at the whole idea of great cities. I doubt that stacking them higher and higher is the answer; we should explore decentralization and I don't mean the fringe suburb. If the jobs stay in the city the suburbanites are chained to the old cities, and the traffic and maintenance programs will become unbearable. I'm talking about settling new towns in the open spaces. We might see how far the people would move if the job moved with them."

This is the long run. How about the short and frightful run of riots and racism, burn, baby, burn? He is suddenly quite calm. "Once we have violence, we've got to have enforce-ment—prompt and certain. We've been lacking in enforce-ment. The criminal must know he'll be punished at once." He is so clear and unspeculative about this that we don't pur-sue the toughening procedures of the Oakland police or the questionable threats of Mayor Yorty of Los Angeles to crack down with force on all malefactors or apparent malefactors when the trouble starts.

And supposing he had to declare himself on the election issues for 1968? "Vietnam may not be there, but if it is it'll be issue number one. Either way the great issue is an umbrella issue, what I call the Morality Gap: crime, obscenity, delin-quency, and abandonment of law. Demonstrations must be within the limits of civil disobedience. Labor and student dis-putes should start with negotiations, not, my God, with a strike. Now, they all take to the streets at once."

You leave him having gained an impression of an engaging kind of energy. He is precise and thoughtful on finance and the mechanics of welfare, quietly dogmatic about the social ferment. He talks no jargon, which is a rare relief. He chants few slogans. he does not preach or intone. He sounds like a decent, deadly serious, baffled middle-class professional man. This, as an executive geared for social rebellion and re-form, may be his weakness. But it is his strength among the voters that, in a country with a huge middle class, he so faithfully reflects their bewilderment at the collapse of the old, middle-class standards, protections, and, perhaps, shibboleths.

16

The Duke

(1974)

When it is finished," says the guidebook, "it may well be the largest cathedral in the world." I am always leery of sentences that contain "may well be." But it is certainly a very large cathedral, namely, the Episcopal Cathedral Church of St. John the Divine on the Upper West Side in New York City. Its foundations were laid in 1892. They've been building it ever since, and the end is not yet.

On Monday, May 27, 1974, St. John the Divine housed a ceremony that would have flabbergasted its architect and its early worshipers. Every pew was filled, and the aisles were choked, and there were several thousands listening to loudspeakers out on the street. And when the ten thousand people inside were asked to stand and pray, there was a vast rustling sound as awesome, it struck me, as that of the several million bats whooshing out of the Carlsbad Caverns in New Mexico at the first blush of dusk.

It is not the size of the crowd that would have shocked the cathedral's founders (they might have taken it jubilantly as a sign of a great religious revival). It was what the crowd was there for. A crowd that ranged through the whole human color scale, from the most purple black to the most pallid white, come to honor the life and mourn the death of a man who had become supreme in an art that began in the brothels of New Orleans. The art is that of jazz, and the practitioner of it they mourned was Edward Kennedy Ellington, identified around the world more immediately than any member of any royal family as—the Duke.

The Duke's career was so much his life that there's very little to say about his private ups and downs, if any. He was born in Washington, D.C., in 1890, the son of a White House butler, and perhaps the knowledge that Father had a special, protected status inside the white Establishment had much to do with the Duke's seeming to be untouched, or untroubled, by the privations and public humiliations we should expect of a black born in the nation's capital. Certainly he must have thought of himself as belonging to one of the upper tiers of black society. But his upbringing could be called normal for any of the black boys who were to turn into great jazzmen. I'm thinking of men like Earl Hines and Fats Waller, the sons of colored parsons or church organists, who, almost automatically as little boys, were hoisted onto a piano stool. The Duke took piano lessons, but also took to sketching and thought of a career as an artist. This dilemma was solved by his becoming a sign painter by day and running small bands by night.

What got him going was the nightly grind and the daily practice. It is something that nightclub habitués seldom credit, it being assumed that while classical pianists must follow a daily regimen, people like Ellington, Hines, Waller, Tatum, simply have a "natural gift" and just rattle the stuff off on request. Nothing could be more false. I remember ten or fifteen years ago running into an old and engaging jazzman, a white who was employed in a poky little jazz joint in San Francisco. Muggsy Spanier was a sweet and talented man who had had a long experience of the roller-coaster fortunes of a jazzman: one year you are playing before delirious crowds in a movie theater or grand hotel, three years later blowing your brains out before a few listless drunks in a crummy roadhouse off the main highway in some place called Four Forks, Arkansas, or New Iberia, Louisiana. Just then Muggsy was in a lean year playing in a small band with Earl Hines, who was also at a low ebb (this was before Hines, the father of jazz piano, had been discovered by the State Department and the Soviet government, or been rediscovered by a new generation). Well, Muggsy had left his trumpet in this dreadful nightclub and found he needed it, on his night off, for some impromptu gig or other. So he had to go into the nightclub next morning, always a depressing experience, what with the reek of sour air and spilled alcohol and the lights turned down to a maintenance bulb or two. He told me that one of the unforgettable shocks of his stint in San Francisco was coming from the bone-white sunlight into the smelly cave and squinting through the dark and seeing Hines sitting there, as he did for two or three hours every morning, practicing not the blues or "Rosetta" or "Honey-suckle Rose" but the piano concertos of Mozart and Beethoven. To the gaping Muggsy, Hines looked up and said, "Just keeping the fingers loose." To be the best, it's a sad truth most of us amateurs shrink from admitting, you have to run, fight, golf, write, play the piano every day. I think it was Paganini—it may have been Rubinstein—who said: "If I go a week without practice, the audience notices it. If I go a day without practice, I notice it."

This digression is very relevant to the character and the mastery of Duke Ellington. He was at a piano, but he was there as a composer, day in and night out. For a man of such early and sustained success, it is amazing that he not only tolerated the grind, after one-night stands, of the long bus rides through the day, and the pickup meals, but actually cherished them as the opportunity to sit back and scribble and hum and compose. He did this to the end.

I knew all the records of his first period when I was in college, from 1927 through 1932. And when I first arrived in New York I wasted no time in beating it up to the Cotton Club to see the great man in the flesh. But, apart from a nodding acquaintance in nightclubs, and becoming known to him no doubt as one of those ever-present nuisances who request this number and that, I didn't meet Ellington alone, by appointment so to speak, until the very end of the Second War. I went up to his apartment on the swagger side of Harlem. There is such a place, in fact there are as many fine shadings of Negro housing through the hierarchy of Negro social status as there are shadings of pigment from the high yaller to the coal black. Ellington was at the top of the scale, in a large Victorian building looking out on a patch of greenery.

The date had been set for two in the afternoon. In my mind's eye I had the picture complete: the dapper figure of the Duke seated in a Noël Coward bathrobe deep in composition at a concert grand. For those were the days long before bandleaders got themselves in gold lamé and sequins. The big bandleaders wore dinner jackets. The Duke wore white tie and tails, and was as sleek as a seal.

Well, I was shown into a large and rambling apartment with a living room that had evidently seen a little strenuous drinking the night before. Off from the living room behind curtained French doors was a bedroom. The doors were open and there in full view was a large bed rumpled and unmade. Beyond that was a bathroom, and out of it emerged what I first took to be some swami in the wrong country. It was the Duke, naked except for a pair of underdrawers and a towel woven around his head. He came in groaning slightly and saying to himself, "Man!" Then *his* man came in, his butler, and they went into the knotty question of what sort of breakfast would be at once tasty and medicinal. It was agreed on, and the Duke turned and said, "Now." Meaning what's your business at this unholy hour of two in the afternoon?

The breakfast arrived and he went at it like a marooned mountaineer. To my attempts to excite him with the proposal I had come to make, he grunted "Uh-huh" and "Un-un" between, or during, mouthfuls.

At last he pushed the plate away, picked up his coffee cup, and sat down and slurped it rapidly and nodded for me to begin again. I had come to suggest that he might like to record a long session with his band for the BBC. This was, remember, the peak period of his big band, and I suggested that we record him not, as we now say, "in concert," but in rehearsal. He shot a suspicious glare at me, as if I'd suggested recording him doing five-finger exercises. But slowly and wearily he began to see my problem, and to respect it. Simply, how to convey to a listener (this was before television) the peculiar genius of the Duke, since it was unique in the practice of jazz music. Which was somehow to be, and feel, present at the act of creation when it was happening to the Duke standing in front of the band in rehearsal. Everybody knows that the best jazz is impossible to write down in the usual musical notation. You can no more make a transcription of Hines playing "I Can't Give You Anything but Love" or, worse, Art Tatum playing any of his cascading variations on "Tea for Two," than you can write down three rules for the average swimmer to follow in doing the two hundred meters like Mark Spitz. Jazz is always improvisation done best by a group of players who know each other's whimsical ways with such mysteries as harmonics, counterpoint, scooped pitch, jamming in unison. Alone among jazz composers, the Duke's raw material was the tune, scribbled bridge passages, a sketch in his head of the progression of solos and ensembles he wanted to hear, and an instinctive knowledge of the rich and original talents, and strengths and perversities, of his players. They were not just trumpet, trombone, clarinet, E-flat alto sax and so on. They were individual performers who had stayed with him for years, for decades. One of them, Harry Carney, played with the Duke on his first recording date in 1927, and he was with him on the last date, in Kalamazoo, Michigan, last March. In 1927 Ellington had created a weird, compact, entirely personal sound with his band. It was weirder still and richer, but it was just as personal at the end.

Eventually the Duke appreciated that what we wanted was not just another performance. He agreed, and we had a long and unforgettable session, in a hired studio on Fifth Avenue, where we recorded the whole process of the number dictated, the roughest run-through with many pauses, trying this fusion of instruments and that, stopping and starting and transferring the obligato from one man to another, the Duke talking and shouting, "Now, Tricky, four bars" and "Barney, in there eight." And in the last hour, what had been a taste in the Duke's head came out as a harmonious, rich meal.

The Duke was nicknamed as a boy by a friend who kidded him about his sharp dressing. He was an elegant and articulate man and, as I've hinted, strangely apart from the recent turmoil of his race. Not, I think, because he was ever indifferent or afraid. He was a supremely natural man, and in his later years devout, and he seemed to assume that men of all colors are brothers. And most of the immediate problems of prejudice and condescension and tension between black and white dissolved in the presence of a man whom even an incurable bigot must have recognized as a man of unassailable natural dignity. He had a childlike side, which—we ought to remember—is recommended in the New Testament for entry into the kingdom of Heaven. He was very sick indeed in the last few months. He knew, but kept it to himself, that he had cancer in both lungs. A week or two before the end, he sent out to hundreds of friends and acquaintances what looked at first like a Christmas card. It was a greeting. On a field of blue was a cross, made up of four vertical letters and three horizontal. They were joined by the letter O. The vertical word spelled "Love" and the horizontal "God."

He has left us, in the blessed library of recorded sound, a huge anthology of his music from his twenty-eighth birthday to his seventy-fifth. He began as a minority cult, too rude or difficult for the collectors of dance music. For much, maybe most, of his time he was never a best-seller. He never stuck in the current groove, or in his own groove. He moved with all the influences of the time, from blues to bebop and the moderns, and transmuted them into his own, and at the end his difficult antiphonies and plotted discords, the newer harmonic structures he was always reaching for, were no more saleable to the ordinary popular-music fan than they had ever been. Most people simply bowed to him as to an institution.

In 1931 a college roommate of mine who was something of a pioneer as a jazz critic, on the university weekly, was graduating, and he wrote a farewell piece. He recorded the rise and fall—during his four-year stint—of the Red Hot Peppers and the Blue Four and McKinney's Cotton Pickers and Bix and Trumbauer. He ended with the phrase: "Bands may come and bands may go, but the Duke goes on forever." Ah, how true! We thought it a marvel that the Duke had ridden out all fashions for four long years. In fact, his good and always developing music lasted for forty-seven years. And we have it all.

So I am inclined to paraphrase what John O'Hara said on the death of George Gershwin: "Duke Ellington is dead. I don't have to believe it if I don't want to."

17

Aiken of Vermont

(1982)

By November, up here in Vermont, the scarlet and gold landscape of the fall has usually faded into russet, and at regular intervals around winding roads there are pyramids of burning leaves like smoldering camp fires. But Thanksgiving Day 1984 was, by Vermonters' lights, marvelously brilliant and beautiful, a flashback. It was cold, not as cold as it will be by January ("7 A.M., 23 degrees below zero and all is well") but sharp, what Dickens called "piping cold." The sun had risen in an orange glow and would go down later, as the song says, in blood.

In the early afternoon, it was a brisk, almost playful sight: all these hurrying bundled-up people, like a jolly Brueghel festival, dipping over the green mountains and bobbing across the valleys to the great American family feast.

This year's Thanksgiving was special in Vermont, for a special family reason. For once, pride in the death of a famous son went beyond the usual media slop and boilerplate rhetoric into a truth people knew and felt. Even though the day was glittering and most people outdoors seemed as cheerful as they are meant to be on that day, from every public building throughout the state, and from the bedroom windows of the smallest rural cottage, the flags were at half-mast—for a man whose life and character moved in a straight line, from a small farm to a big farm, to the state legislature, to the governorship and then, forty-three years ago, to the Senate of the United States, where he remained a gathering force for many tough good things. A funny, independent, Yankee-shrewd, totally incorruptible man, who went back home to Vermont in his eighty-fourth year. Until only a few months ago, his sense and experience were available to anybody who cared to tap them. Then he failed quickly and died—at ninety-two. Senator George D. Aiken. So, on Thanksgiving Day, at the funeral in the small town he grew up in, there was little cause for mourning at the grave.

George Aiken was a type we like to think will be always with us. Vermont is a mountainous, landlocked state between New Hampshire and upstate New York. Deceptively beautiful, for just beneath its rolling green carpet is very rocky terrain, which—combined with great extremes of temperature—restricts its farming to dairying (lots of cows) and fruit-growing. Indeed, the value of its farm crops is such as to leave it the second poorest farming state in the Union. But, because of its production of fine marble, and building stone; because of a prosperous industry in the syrup that's tapped from its forests of maples; because of a thriving skiing industry; because, also, in a state bigger than Wales, there are only half a million people, there is less poverty than most places.

The Aikens were among the original English settlers on this forbidding soil. The French had set up sparse settlements there in the seventeenth century, but the first English came in in the 1740s, and came for keeps. I go back so far, because in 1773, one Edward Aiken, on a journey far from home, was suddenly taken ill. A stranger who took him in got the word slowly, by mountain scout and stage, to his wife, who thereupon put herself and her youngest child on a horse and rode just on a hundred miles to nurse her husband. This is the sort of family memory that George Aiken would acknowledge but not go on about.

He was born in 1892 and from babyhood on was brought up in the village of Putney, a place unknown outside the state but one that shocked the world in the early 1840s, when a man named John Noyes started a religious movement he called "Perfectionism." It entailed having property in common, households in common, and wives in common. He called this idea Complex Marriage. He's forgotten now, but he did earn the dubious reward of a compliment from George Bernard Shaw, who described the Putney experiment as "one of those chance attempts at Superman which occur from time to time, in spite of the interference of man's blundering institutions." Well, Complex Marriage was too complex for the people of Putney. Noyes fled into New York State, and the Vermonters blundered on, and the Aikens kept their one farm, and several children—by one wife.

George Aiken never got beyond high school. After that, he

borrowed a hundred dollars and planted a raspberry patch, which five years later he extended to five hundred acres. And it was all his. He went into the commercial cultivation of fruits and wildflowers. He was forty-two before he moved on into state politics, first in the legislature and then on to the governorship. The governors of Vermont have—like members of the United States House of Representatives—only two years in which to leave their mark, and most of them are remembered by the locals, so to speak, for the good or bad things they did *in* the state. Governor Aiken's name, however, attracted much attention outside Vermont when, during the Depression, he proposed that neighboring states ought to band together to build publicly owned generating stations to provide low-cost power, for farmers especially. This was taken as a declaration of war against private industry, and many of his own party were shocked that such a proposal should come from a Republican. You can see how, when Aiken got to Washington, the Roosevelt New Dealers laid down the red carpet for this independent Republican when they launched their offensive against the private utilities, and Congress set up the huge public power project of the Tennessee Valley Authority. Bowing to the compliment but remaining his own man, he was no party's captive. When President Roosevelt started the whole business of subsidizing farmers' crops across the board—across the land—both Republican and Democratic senators from farming states fell gratefully into the president's arms. Aiken thought it a bad principle that would get farmers into the habit of being subsidized in bad times and good, a habit by now so ingrained that even the most free-enterprising Republican presidents have come to assume that farm subsidies are an American birthright.

In the Senate, Aiken made his mark during his first term but for a long time it was, to his party's chieftains, the mark of an unreliable, a loner. For instance, he had the idea that one way to keep scrimping families above the poverty line was to have the federal government give away not cash benefits but food stamps!—a bizarre idea, which took twenty years to become government policy.

To many senators, George Aiken was simply an old-fashioned Yankee eccentric. In one thing eccentric to the point of dementia: promptly at the end of every financial year he sent to the Treasury a check for the part of his office allowance he had never used. Also while it is quite proper and normal for a senator's wife to work in his office as a paid assistant, when Aiken married his administrative assistant, she stayed on in her job but he took her off the payroll. He not only, like legions of Republicans, believed in thrift. He practiced it.

He dearly loved his work on the Senate's Public Welfare Committee, but when the senior Republican post on the Foreign Relations Committee fell vacant, he took it, because otherwise it would have been filled by a man he quietly detested: Senator Joseph McCarthy.

I wish it were possible to quote from the spate of dry, wry one-liners he got off in a lifetime of marvelous, deadpan speeches. But he wrote few of them down. You had to be there when he remarked about Congress that "I have never seen so many incompetent persons in high office." When he answered the familiar charge against his party that the Republicans were "me-tooers," it would do what the Democrats did but do it better. "Let's," he said, "not be afraid of the 'me-too' charge. If a Democrat comes out for better health, I'm not going to come out for poorer health."

I recall a dinner speech he made during the presidential campaign year of 1980, when half a dozen Republican aspirants were barging and bellowing through New Hampshire and Vermont. There was a rumor went rustling around that one of them, an eminent governor, had blunted charges of looking too old by dyeing his hair. Aiken chided the dinner company: "While he is here as a candidate, political criticism is proper, but he is a guest of the state and personal remarks are out of place." He paused before a thoughtful aside: "At the same time, I have to admit that in all my years in Washington, I can't remember another politician whose hair turned orange overnight!" In 1966, when America was beginning to get deep into the Vietnam War, he advised President Johnson: "Declare the United States the winner, and get out." It took eight years for America to do it.

He will be publicly remembered for public power; for the St. Lawrence Seaway; for bucking Joseph McCarthy; for the Food Stamp Act. By three generations of the neighbors who knew him, he will be remembered for his upright walk and ways, his shambling clothes and windblown hair, for his charm, his dry humor, and the fact that he could never be bought. George Aiken of Vermont. Not, let us hope, a vanished type.

18

Barbara McClintock:
The Gene on the Cob
(1983)

The front page of the newspaper had been folded over, so that what I first saw was the top half, which carried a photograph of a sweet old lady with a face like an apple wearing granny glasses. The name and the caption were hidden from view, and I had to guess who she was and what she was doing there.

I resisted the natural impulse to open up the paper and find out because, only an evening or two before, I had played a game with some friends that challenged this very ability to determine character and profession from the evidence of an uncaptioned photograph. The game was provoked by the assertion of an old friend, a veteran politician watcher, that in identifying character from photographs, we are the victims of eighty years of the movies' power to impose stereotypes. The mere suggestion that intelligent and literate beings like us had had their view of character dictated by a casting director so inflamed the self-respect of several guests (and the "self-esteem" of a feminist present) that at once a neutral, disinterested host was chosen to go off, riffle through a variety of magazines and newspapers and clip from them a dozen photographs of men and women in the news, none of them sufficiently well-known to be recognizable to anyone in our group. Some, perhaps, were famous in their own countries. Most were, to us at any rate, anonymous.

Each numbered photo was pasted on a large sheet of paper and put down on a table we were sitting around. Alongside the photo gallery was placed another sheet bearing a list, unnumbered, of the trade or profession of each of the characters on display. The game was, of course, to match the face and the profession.

At the end, I don't believe anyone had a much better score than twenty—twenty-five—percent. The sort of thing the group was faced with was the revelation that number 6—chosen by three people as a French novelist and by one as a surgeon—was, in fact, a Chicago truck driver, representing the Teamsters. A face confidently assigned by several of us to the one murderer on the list was a judge on the International Court of Justice at The Hague. And so on. The moral is surely no subtler than that contained in two famous tags: "We see in a work of art what we bring to it"—and more to the point, as Shakespeare usually is—"There is no art to find the mind's construction in the face."

So before I unfolded that morning newspaper to know who was the little old lady (the apple wearing glasses) I immediately guessed she was the brave grandmother of a marine killed in Lebanon or—no!—perhaps the latest winner of a million-dollar lottery, the beneficiary of some ludicrous stroke of luck which alone could put such a modest, old, midwestern, rural face on the front page of the *New York Times*. She was, she is, Barbara McClintock, only the third woman in history to have won the Nobel Prize for science.

There is nothing condescending or cute in calling her a "little old lady." She is five feet high, weighs seven stone (ninety-eight pounds) and is eighty-one. You can see her type, her physical type, any day on the tube: in commercials for Grandma Mary Lou's Bran Muffins—or telling us, with great sweetness and glinting glasses, what Deepdown, the magic ointment, has done for her arthritis.

The mention that Miss McClintock (she's a lifelong spinster) is eighty-one and the winner of this year's Nobel Prize for medicine will set a lot of people to wondering what happened to the theory, which is confirmed by generations of pioneer scientists, that the basic discoveries in any science have been made by people in their late twenties, early thirties at the latest. Barbara McClintock doesn't exactly give the lie to it. Forty years ago, she had evolved and proved to her own satisfaction the theory that won her the prize. But, she confessed cheerfully the other day, speaking of the scientists, the foundations, the journals she wanted to pass on her discovery to: "They thought I was crazy, absolutely mad." She had published her results, but they were either ignored or ridiculed. "Nobody was reading me," she said, "so what was the use?" She gave up publishing, not in bitterness or disdain. She was sure of her ground and she went on quietly every day breeding corn on the cob. How's that? Yes, what this continent calls corn and the other English-speaking peoples call maize. She's been mooching around her little corn patch on Long Island ever since.

Before we come to that, we ought to go back to her beginnings and how she came on this extraordinary, or astonishingly ordinary, specialty. She was (like Katharine Hepburn) the daughter of a doctor in Hartford, Connecticut. Against her mother's conventional belief—at the time—that no respectable girl went to college, she went off at the age of seventeen to Cornell University. But then, in this country, a lot of girls were going to college before and during the First World War. The great majority of them went to polish up their general culture with an arts degree. But this determined midget had a weird interest—plant breeding, an impossible undergraduate specialty—so she took botany. Fifty-five years ago, she earned a doctor of science degree in plant genetics, and from then on devoted her life to maize. It was a time when women were rarely, if ever, taken on as full-time staff lecturers at a university. So she moved around for fifteen years, until a philanthropic foundation offered her a more or less permanent job at a small lab, a genetics lab on Long Island, where she's been ever since.

That was in 1942. Her true laboratory was not a sterilized sanctuary gleaming with retorts and bubbling with noxious liquids. It was a patch of grass outside on which she grew her corn. The small, the jealous, world of geneticists heard about her unflinching dedication to this odd specialty and elected her to the National Academy of Sciences on the assumption that sooner or later she would come through with some eminently respectable research along known lines. Well, she didn't. After nine years of growing and planting and pollinating and watching and thinking, she announced her discovery, which she was convinced went beyond her observations of corn cobs. She said that genes are not fixed units, planted in a permanent position on the chromosome. She said they jump around according to no predictable plan, so that the color changes in a kernel of maize cannot be explained by a known pattern of heredity. They obey the command of some sort of switch, and move from one part of a chromosome to another at the bidding of yet another element known as an activator.

I imagine that this knotty theory is beyond most of us, but at the time even people in the genetic know thought it a fairly preposterous theory. As a Nobel Committee member said: "The trouble was, in 1951, only about five people in the world could possibly know what she was talking about." So— like Mr. Toots hearing that the love of his life had turned him down—she said, "It's of no account, thank 'ee" and for thirty more years went about her daily business with corn cobs, not caring much what the experts thought. "When you know you're right," she said the other day, "you know that sooner or later it will come out in the wash."

Well, it took a great deal more biological and chemical research, by many people in many places, before the wash revealed that, for example, bacteria that become resistant to an antibiotic pass on to other bacteria the resistant strain, by way of—guess what?—Barbara McClintock's crazy switches and activators. Two years ago only, in 1981, the world of science received the wake-up call as it might an earthquake and rushed to acknowledge her as a great and, if you'll excuse the word, long-neglected pioneer. Medical awards and money came pouring in with apologetic speed. And, two weeks ago, the Nobel Prize. She has no telephone, so she happened to hear it on the radio. She had no idea, and didn't seem to care much, what the prize was worth in cash. A reporter told her: "One hundred and ninety thousand dollars." "Dear me," she said.

19

George Abbott

(1995)

One time, years ago, the veteran Baltimore newspaper-man, H. L. Mencken, was checking copy coming in from the night editor and sighing at the rising number of errors he was noticing, errors of fact but also of syntax, and even some idioms that didn't sound quite right. He shook his head and said, as much to himself as to the editor at his side: "The older I get the more I admire and crave competence, just simple competence, in any field from adultery to zoology."

Maybe this complaint is, like arthritis, a normal compan-ion of advancing years, like Socrates' lament over the bad manners of the young. But, at a given time, it may also be true for a given skill. Thirty years ago, two old painters painted and glazed the walls of my study, and nothing has had to be done to them since. I have to say that the skill of their successors in the rest of the apartment has been slap-happy by comparison.

What made me zoom in on the idea of competence, however, was the death the other day of a man who, more than any other single person I can recall—male, female or hermaphrodite—represented an American institution at its most competent. He was not a genius, not an innovator, not a landmark talent. It could well be that none of his works in the years to come will ever be revived. Simply, a totally competent professional. The name is George Abbott. And the institution he glorified and came almost to symbolize was—Broadway. Oddly, along that brassy, nonchalant street, he bore no nickname, which was a tribute to his appearance. There was something about him: a natural dignity, a dour quizzical face (he would have made a marvelous Scrooge) that did not invite familiarity. Six feet two, he stood like a grenadier. He never, ever, wore a sports shirt or other off-duty clothes. Always a gray suit, white shirt and necktie everywhere, in the hottest weather. He was known to actors, producers, sponsors, directors, designers, cast, young and old—to all but a tiny circle of close friends—as "Mr. Abbott." He didn't request or expect this formality. He might have liked to be called George by one and all. Once, indeed, to a young protégé, he did say, "Please call me George." The young man said, "I certainly will, Mr. Abbott."

Like several other famous ones who came to appear as the essence or spirit of a certain place or kind of life, he was brought up far from it. Remember Frederic Remington, who in a short life sculpted and drew and painted more horses and Indians and cowboys than anybody in history? He was born in New York and studied at Yale. And how about that shambling boy from a mining town in the Rockies—with the prison haircut and the prairie twang who wore canary yellow shoes and was probably the first man to be said to dress like an unmade bed? Harold Ross, the founder-editor of *The New Yorker,* who sounded a new note of urbanity in American journalism.

Well, Mr. Abbott was, to be truthful, born in rural upstate New York but when he was barely in his teens his parents whisked him off to Cheyenne, Wyoming, a new town, only twenty years old, one of the towns created by the Union Pacific railroad, which indeed claimed the site and laid out the streets parallel to the tracks. It was named after a neighboring tribe by a Union general, Major General Grenville Dodge, who was then chief engineer of the Union Pacific. Pretty soon it was a hive for the regular three types of pioneers: the people who went west meaning to settle; the people who drifted west to feed and house them; and the bigger horde that saw in every settlement a glittering prospect of exploitation—real estate and land speculators, traveling salesmen turning into shopkeepers, craftsmen, gamblers, con men and (as everywhere out west where single men came to roost) what became primly known as ladies of the evening.

In his mid-teens, George Abbott became a Western Union messenger boy when the company was as chic and new as a CD-ROM. One of his first regular jobs was delivering beer to the red light district (a trade known in New Orleans as "the can rusher," which the pimp and bawdy-house piano player Jelly Roll Morton boasted of as his first paid—meaning honorable—job). Every summer, young Abbott went off to work on a ranch, need I say a working ranch—there was no such thing as a dude ranch in those days. It was a constant marvel to Mr. Abbott's friends in later life to hear genuine western stories from the only cowboy they ever knew.

In most of the early towns out west, elementary education was provided by a small, one- or two-room schoolhouse. It was rudimentary but evidently sound, for it always amazes superior city folks, if they ever stop to think, how many soldiers, statesmen and politicians who never went beyond the "little red schoolhouse" came to write and talk a decent serviceable prose. But if the settler parents wanted their sons to move on to high school, they usually had to be sent some distance away to a school that had been started as an adjunct or extension of the forts that the army had built during the Indian wars. Abbott was sent off to such a one, the Kearney Military Academy in Nebraska, the remnant of a fort abandoned once the Sioux had been conquered or dispersed and the railroad had displaced the wagon train.

A more unlikely training for a Broadway producer-director it is hard to imagine, but George Abbott maintained (rarely, and then only to an intimate friend) that what he picked up in the West and never lost was a habit of staying with any job he started and keeping one eye cocked over his shoulder for the man behind who—as the immortal old ballplayer said— "might be gaining on you." All he got out of the military school was, he said, a cure for his chronic stoop.

When he was seventeen, the family moved back east and settled in a small town near Buffalo, New York. He went off to college at Rochester, played a lot of football but on a sudden and never-explained impulse he became hopelessly stagestruck, joined the university dramatic club and spent every penny he earned attending the local theater. After graduation, he had only one aim: to get to Harvard, the only university in the East that had started a course in playwriting. He stayed there until, at the age of twenty-five, he won the prize for his first play, *The Man in the Manhole*. Within the year, he was bound for Broadway and the certain conviction that he would storm the place. But, like many another dazzling amateur, he had a lean time of it for many years, doing every sort of job, slowly rising from office boy to prompter to stage manager, casting director, somebody called "assistant playwright," who was really an apprentice play doctor. Not until he was thirty-six did he find a role that helped him to a steady living. It was that of Tex, a cowboy! But soon after that he wrote and directed his first great hit, called appropriately *Broadway*. Ever afterwards, he could have his choice of scripts. And once he began to pick and choose, he responded to an itch that was never cured: an irresistible desire to doctor scenes, dialogue, even whole plays. He pounced on an original script as raw meat for his butchering. No script satisfied him until he had revised it, rewritten it, dolled it up or dressed it down: an occupation that made him unpopular with some famous playwrights.

So, for the next sixty-three years, from 1926 to 1989, he directed or produced or was somehow involved in over a hundred and twenty productions. When he was ninety-nine, he sent off to a secretary, to retype, two plays he'd written in between rounds of golf. Holidays, by the way, he didn't believe in, he looked on them as a form of defeat. The great thing was to keep on doing what you do best and draw a breath in between shows.

He held no doctrines about how to live, but he was, for a deep-dyed theater man, an oddity. He took three meals a day at regular intervals. He never smoked. He sipped a little wine. He went home early to bed, to read a play, to fiddle with a play, to sleep, to get up and start again. Night life he thought was "a dandy way to get a nervous breakdown." He admitted to certain unchanging prejudices. He liked unknown actors. He had little time for the tantrums of established stars, though the roster of young people spotted by him and then established as stars—from Leonard Bernstein to Shirley MacLaine and Barbra Streisand—is formidable.

He had few theories about stage direction and was willing to listen, for a time. Like Winston Churchill, he believed in reasonable discussion "provided it ended in compliance with my wishes." He couldn't abide the so-called Method actors, who were spawned in the late 1940s, flourished through the 1950s and 1960s and still haunt the more strenuous "psychological" scripts. Mr. Abbott's objection to the school was that a man strained and sweated to imagine himself as an old spinster or, perhaps, an old armchair, but all the while, Mr. Abbott complained, "he can't pronounce his final 't's." One actor, wrestling over the inner meaning of his part, asked "What is my motivation?" "Your job," said Mr. Abbott.

He lost his second wife in 1951 and for thirty-two years he was mostly alone. But twelve years ago, when he was ninety-six, he decided to marry again, a youngster in her early fifties. Last year he came into New York from his house up the river and pattered down the aisle at a revival of his *Damn Yankees,* just to be sure they were pronouncing their final t's. Last week, he was busy at this favorite occupation, tinkering with, rewriting and revising a revival of *Pajama Game.* This week, he died in his sleep at a hundred and seven.

A dozen years ago, he had to have a pacemaker. He had a lifelong suspicion of doctors and their wizardry, and he wanted to know if there was "any snag to this thing." Only, replied the doctor with well-rehearsed facetiousness, "that you'll have to have a new battery after ten years." "Hot damn!" said Mr. Abbott. Ten years later, when he was a hundred and five, sure enough he had to have a new battery. "Hot damn!" said Mr. Abbott, his chronic suspicion of doctors confirmed yet again.

One day, in his late nineties, he was playing golf with his wife and for the first time, and who knows, perhaps the last, fell down on the fairway. In alarm his wife ran over to him, saw the long lean figure still prostrate and shouted: "George! George! Get up, please. Don't just lay there." He opened an eye. "*Lie* there!" he said.

20

Scotty Reston:
The Maestro from Glasgow
(1995)

James Barrett Reston, who came to be called, and rightly, the most influential American journalist of his generation, was at his birth the unlikeliest candidate for influence of any kind in the great world outside Scotland's Clydebank and its sprawling shipyards, where his father worked as a machinist.

Life in the first decade of the twentieth century held out few pleasant prospects for the people who in those honest days were classified in the official census as "the laboring poor," not as "the economically challenged." Yet from across the Atlantic the word from a friend already emigrated suggested that the promise of American life was, at worst, less bleak.

The young Reston was no more than a baby when his parents decided, like the impoverished Andrew Carnegie (often cited by disheartened Scots as a model), to seek the good life in the American Midwest. They pooled their precious small savings, booked the steerage passage, Mrs. Reston and her sister sewed the gold sovereigns into their corsets, and they sailed away. But during the voyage, the sister fell ill, and when they landed at Ellis Island was taken aside to be looked over by one of the doctors, the instant diagnosticians who inscribed fatal chalk marks on sick arrivals (H for suspected heart disease, T for tuberculosis). Whatever the sister's affliction, it was serious enough to have the family denied entry and be forced to make the long journey home. Again they started to put aside sovereigns, but any hopes they had of using them were blasted for four years at least by "the guns of August" and the coming of the so-called Great War.

They stayed home in Clydebank in what young Reston, no sentimentalist, was later to admit could be fairly called "dire" poverty, until the war was over. In 1919, they tried again. This time they were all, including Mrs. Reston's sister, in visibly good health. They passed through Ellis Island and settled in Dayton, Ohio, where Reston senior went to work in an automobile factory.

The mere mention of Dayton recalls for me a remarkable newspaper photograph I saw years ago and have longed for ever since. It was almost certainly a presidential campaign picture (the year was 1920) and showed two tall, affable men, one of them remarkably handsome in a rather lofty, upper-crust way. They were standing on the first tee, drivers in hand, about to celebrate the opening of a new country club (not a chosen event that would endear them to voters today). They were the nominees of the Democratic party for the presidential race: Governor Cox of Ohio and his running mate, a former undersecretary of the navy, one Franklin Delano Roosevelt. (I hear a murmur of doubt: Roosevelt playing golf? It would be a year later, up in the family's summer place in Canada, that Roosevelt contracted the dread disease which everyone feared in those summer days, poliomyelitis, and which paralyzed him for life).

What made this photograph forever poignant and comical at the same time was the presence, alongside the strapping young Roosevelt, of an urchin of a caddie hefting a bag the size of himself. He was a twelve-year-old who thereafter would be known everywhere as "Scotty" Reston. It was an early omen, a reflection of his love of the game. In an immigrant of any other nation, this would have been a very odd affection, and I imagine a lot of the neighbors in Dayton must have thought so. At the time, golf was considered, and in the United States it most certainly was, a rich man's pastime. But—what is still news to most Americans—for about four centuries, golf in Scotland has been the pastime of all classes, from Mary, Queen of Scots to her groom, from the loitering heirs of the shipbuilders to the sons of their laboring poor. In fact, the poor started it and it worked its way up.

It was a proud day for his mother when the Clydebank worker's son went off to college, but a scandalous day when, four years later, young Scotty, having made no better than a mediocre mark in everything but "sportswriting," announced that he was going to become a professional golfer. He had picked up money caddying and twice won the Ohio public links championship. However, he reconciled his mother's opposition and his own inclination by becoming a sports journalist. He soon developed a natural gift for a canny, forthright prose and he hopped quickly up the ladder of Associated Press talent. After five years in New York covering every sport, he was sent to London as their chief man to cover Wimbledon and the British Open golf championship. When these events were over, he was asked to stay on and—astonishingly—cover the Foreign Office! It was the late 1930s, a nervous time, with Mussolini having taken over Ethiopia and Hitler gone into Austria and dismembered Czechoslovakia. Somebody must have had extraordinary confidence in this sturdy thirty-year-old, to whom politics at that point in his career was another, possibly more complicated, game. In any case, Reston was quite unfazed by the assignment and the confidence in him was justified.

It quickly appeared that he had a kind of inquisitiveness that is a good reporter's best endowment: not to pretend to know more than you do but to ask the questions a child would ask. The effect on the people who are in charge of things can be remarkable and often remarkably hurtful. The questioner appears not as a recording machine but as an interrogator who wants to hear the home truths that, in the interests of diplomacy or party policy, are better fudged or left for events to reveal. Reston's strength in his early days covering British policy was that he *was* an innocent. The questions that occurred to him were indeed childlike, and it was an unpleasant experience for the Foreign Office press spokesmen. "They seemed to think," he told me years later, "that reporters were there not to find out the news but to copy it out from the Foreign Office releases. In fact, that's what they did think." Reston might be frustrated by this convention but it did not put him off his new assignment; on the contrary, it made him all the more inquisitive and, eventually, absorbed in the whole business of politics. Within the year, he quit the Associated Press and joined the *New York Times*'s London bureau, on the first of September 1939, the day Hitler went into Poland or—as Reston was careful to report Hitler's version— the day the Nazis felt compelled to respond to the sneaky and murderous Polish invasions of German territory.

After that, sports would seldom come into his writing, though for many years he would play a mean caddie's game of golf. From then on, he had two preoccupations: American foreign policy; and the shifts and audacities whereby a man became president of the United States and how, and how effectively, he wielded power.

For the last quarter century of his life he was a columnist, having chosen at the age of sixty to ease up on the reporter's demanding neutral code and relax into his preferences and prejudices. But his great and inimitable days were his years as a reporter, a craft all the more admirable since its rather palpable decline across the Atlantic. This country still, in the dozen or so serious city newspapers, maintains the tradition that struck me the first weeks I lived here: the strict separation, in substance and tone, of the reporting pages from the editorial, the leader, page. My first mentor, H. L. Mencken, made it plain to me when, in 1937, I became a correspondent here: "Since there is no such thing as ideological truth, it follows that to the extent a reporter is a liberal reporter or a conservative reporter, or a Democratic or Communist or

Republican reporter, he is no reporter at all." My own test was, and is, a simple one: you should not know from a good reporter's work how he votes. Apply this to the newspapers of France and Britain, and you may share my fear that they are declining into journals of opinion.

This quality of maintained neutrality, of seeking out the facts and letting them fall where they may, was taken for granted in all the good reporters I knew, as distinct from the columnists and commentators, who knowingly mix analysis and advocacy. What made Reston supreme at his craft was his unflagging hard labor on a job, his tapping never less than three or four sources (some contradictory), his capacity to tunnel for undiscovered facts while the rest of us tended to describe the landscape over the tunnel. Most of all was his enviable gift of wheedling out of officials—not public relations officers or deputy undersecretaries but prime ministers and field marshals and dictators and tycoons and holy men—confessions of things, both pleasant and unpleasant, that had happened. This ready access was due, I think, to his remarkable international prestige but, more likely, to his reputation for not identifying his sources.

He had a marvelous cocky streak which was so amiably, almost jokingly, expressed that it caused no offense to notice but rather a belch of laughter. Once, I recall, we were mulling over the plight of NATO a day or two after de Gaulle pulled France out of it. Scotty sighed, tapped the stem of his pipe against his teeth and said a little wearily, "I think I'd better call on the general." Which, without more fuss than a minute or two over the telephone, he proceeded to arrange.

I have no doubt that a couple of days later he would be flying off to Paris, and while he was over there might just as well drop in on the new Labour prime minister, Harold Wilson.

There was a mythical story, which if not true ought to be, about the king of England's saying, after Britain went off the gold standard, "I shouldn't be surprised if Scotty Reston wasn't behind this whole thing." Certainly, Scotty was one day ahead of our (the *Guardian*'s) financial expert, then in Washington, in reporting that the retreat from gold was *going* to happen. Days before any other paper, the *New York Times* published under Reston's byline the details of the Dumbarton Oaks conference (no reporters present), which laid out, to the astonishment of the men who had been there, the blueprint of the oncoming United Nations.

Most risibly, I remember a Bermuda conference between Macmillan and President Kennedy. Absolutely nothing was coming out of the press officers of either side, and the parties of the first part could not be reached. The day wore on and out, as several hundred of us, seeing no hope of transmitting the communiqué, drifted and sifted and boozed into the night. Scotty was nowhere in sight. Just after eleven, he came in, jaunty with his bosun's roll, a little flushed, a puff of smoke preceding a large grin. He got me off in a corner. I asked him how the canary tasted. He chuckled till he had to wipe away the tears. He took a long happy draw on the pipe. On a promise that I would write nothing till the morrow, he told me what had gone on at the conference, who said what to whom, what the communiqué would say, better—something communiqués are designed to hide—what the communiqué meant. Unlike the stories of most journalists who have just scored a coup, his bore no hint of self-congratulation. It was plain, informative, exactly right, letter perfect. Where'd you get all this from, I asked. He wiped another tear: "I was under the carpet," he said.

He was always under the carpet. This genial, Scots-shrewd, bulky but compact figure, ready for Moscow, Downing Street or the Pentagon, affable, unfooled, gave a special glow to the title reporter. After a bad bout with the grimmest of diseases, he died in 1995, during the anniversary week of Pearl Harbor, full of years and sly, quiet wisdom to the end.

21

Erma Bombeck:
A Rare Bird
(1996)

A beloved woman has just died. I choose the word carefully. The cause of her being loved was a talent, much akin to the genius of Mark Twain, for writing about the daily life of ordinary people without sentimentality, facetiousness or mock tragedy but with a wry sort of candor that called from her audience the response—sometimes delighted, sometimes abashed—"She's right, but that's me!"

In a word, she was something very rare: a woman humorist. If that sounds cavalier or bullying, in a macho way, I'd better say that that was not a flip remark. It is the outcome of years of brain-crunching thought which, in another age, might well have led to the discovery of the law of gravity. As it was, it led me to a simple distinction between wit and humor that has been confirmed every time somebody points out to me yet another funny woman writer. They always turn out to be wits, which goes at once to my theory that whereas wits have a target that is somebody outside themselves, the target of a humorist is himself. At his best he says blankly stupid things with the air of being specially wise, or he confesses a flaw in his character which we at once recognize as one of our own. To put it simply, wits make fun of other people, humorists make fun of themselves.

The most celebrated wit of her time, which was the time of the 1920s and 1930s, was Dorothy Parker. Reviewing Katharine Hepburn's debut as a leading lady on Broadway, she noticed— or pretended to notice—that whenever an old, famous actress, one Blanche Bates, came on stage, Katharine Hepburn retreated into the farthest corner. "Could it be," mused Miss Parker, "that Miss Hepburn was afraid of catching acting from Miss Bates?" We all hoot over such a wounding shaft (Brendan Gill, another wit, called Dorothy Parker's wit "a surgical enterprise") but are greatly relieved not to be the object of it.

On the other hand, consider the deeply thoughtful remark of Mark Twain after he'd been a month or two in England: "The English countryside is too beautiful to be left out of doors; it should be put under glass."

I hope this is enough to show why humorists are lovable, wits never. Think of some of the renowned wits of our century: Bernard Shaw, Ambrose Bierce, Oscar Wilde, Noël Coward, Evelyn Waugh, Gore Vidal. They have been called many things, but lovable is not one of them.

This country seems to abound with witty women, some of them terrifyingly so. Fran Lebowitz is always, and rightly, called "acerbic." I think Florence King may be the funniest writer alive, in the English language, but she is an arch misogynist who hates the human race and writes—not without good cause—books with such apt titles as *Reflections in a Jaundiced Eye* and *With Charity toward None.* I admire her extravagantly, so long as she's whipping other people, but I should hate to have her take off on me.

However, none of this is true of Erma Bombeck, who has just died in San Francisco in her seventieth year. She was a columnist for most of her life and put together several cherished collections, cherished, I should say, by a very large middle-class audience, of women I should guess more than men. Her titles were such as *When You Look Like Your Passport Photo, It's Time to Go Home* and *If Life Is a Bowl of Cherries, Why Am I in the Pits?*

She was born Erma Fiste in a small town in Ohio, German on her father's side. He has been variously described as a crane operator or a construction worker. (Erma would have preferred the older, if less exact, word: bricklayer.) He died of a heart attack when Erma, an only child, was nine, and she and her mother went off to live with a grandmother. At about the age of twelve, she began writing a humorous column for her junior high school paper, got out of high school toward the end of the Second World War, became a copy girl on the nearby big-town newspaper, in Dayton, graduated as a bachelor of arts from that city's university and all in the same year married William Bombeck, a sportswriter who later became a high school headmaster. For her remaining forty-seven years, he was her one and only husband, favorite subject of wonder and (whenever she felt herself mean enough to turn into a wit instead of a humorist) her favorite object!

Her career was that of her generation—brace your-selves!—mother and housewife. She was born too soon to hear, from the savvy young feminists, that "you can have it all": man, children, executive job, law practice. When, later in life, she did hear it, she didn't believe it.

But if that passing wind of change didn't knock her off her pins it left her a touch unsteady. It was the 1960s, and Erma Bombeck was in her thirty-eighth year. One day she was sitting in her kitchen "looking out the window," she wrote, "watching women like Anne Morrow Lindbergh and Golda Meir carving out their own careers, and I decided it wasn't fulfilling enough to stay cleaning water taps with a tooth-brush. I was too young for Social Security, too tired for an affair. I decided it was my time to strike out." The last of her three children were now off at school. "Striking out" meant a daring decision: to write a column—for a newspaper. She persuaded a small suburban newspaper to pay her three dollars a column. "I was on my way," she said. The next year, the editor of the big-city paper, the *Dayton Journal-Herald,* no less, spotted her stuff and made her the fabulous offer of fifteen dollars a week for three columns! She grabbed it. The rest is—worldwide syndication.

Later on, people used to ask her: how did you choose the subject of your column? Simple, she said, "being a housewife was the only thing I could discuss for more than four minutes." That, indeed, is mostly what she did discuss in her columns, for the following thirty-one years. You'd think she must have plowed a grinding, monotonous furrow. It is the predictable fate of most humorists who have to be funny twice a week no matter how they're feeling. But, astonishingly, to the end, Erma Bombeck was rarely mechanical or predictable, even though she was writing about the most familiar domestic joys and woes: husband, children, the measles, kitchen stoves, holidays, yearning for holidays, love of home, boredom with home, fascinations and horrors of teenagers, a husband's capacity to sit immobile watching football ("when a man watches four consecutive football games, he can be declared legally dead")—about her second-favorite household chore, ironing ("my first being banging my head on the bedpost till I faint").

It must be obvious that by the time, almost twenty years ago, she was syndicated in more than nine hundred newspapers around the world, she had long ago ceased to be a household slave, or what we used to call a housewife, though she blithely used the title to the end. She earned something short of a million dollars a year for many years, and for the last two decades had lived in a valley out west, in the Arizona desert. So most of her later stuff, the themes of maybe three-quarters of her output, were exercises in remembrance of things past. But they were never memories recalled in the luxury of later life. Until the last year, when she was very ill, she did her own shopping, all but the heaviest housework, she checked the price tags on everything; and when her illness began to overwhelm her, she kept up her spirits with odd recollections and instant jokes about marriage in all its stages. She banged out what came to mind, and it caused the joy of chuckling or the wince of recognition especially in her huge, far-flung audience of women: on dirty ovens ("If it won't catch fire today, clean it tomorrow"); on sibling rivalry ("Who gets the ice cream sundae with the lone cherry on top?"); a warning to wives—"The light in the refrigerator is blinding to the male of the species." Women, she reflected, especially married women, never cease fantasizing: "All over the country housewives are fantasizing their husbands taking the kids to the fair or something and leaving them alone for four days . . . the other day, an exterminator knocked on my door asking for directions, and I wondered—'Is he the one?'"

If Erma Bombeck is the only woman humorist (I'm eager to receive other applications), you may wonder why this should be so. Well, as I said in another way at the beginning, there are enough talented men who are secure in the scheme of things to feel free to make fun of themselves. I don't believe that in our civilization women have yet achieved sufficient sense of emotional equality to be eager to help men make fun of them. By the complementary reason, all the funny women I know are wits—all too grateful for their ability to strike back.

So why now should Erma Bombeck appear? It is a puzzle, but I hazard a solution. She was, from the accounts of all her friends, a winning, happy woman. She watched her husband with steady affection, so often the stumbling victim of her pieces, but she was confident enough of her own fallibility to make herself an equal butt. I believe this happy balance was due first to her temperament, a sanguine temperament, allied to her God-given gift (she wrote as simply as St. Luke: "And the word went out that all the world was to be taxed.

The Democrats won again!"). The happy state of her marriage gave the gift and the temperament together free rein to express her humor. Twenty-five years ago, she told an interviewer: "The good years of my life began with my marriage. The rest has been gravy."

22

The Last Victorian
(1983)

CHURCHILL, WINSTON LEONARD SPENCER: Statesman, soldier, journalist, amateur bricklayer and painter. Nobel Prize for Literature, 1963. Knighted, 1953.

b. Nov. 30, 1874 in the ladies' cloakroom of Blenheim Palace, to Lady Randolph Churchill (b. Jennie Jerome, New York City), who, against her doctor's orders, was attending a ball. Son of Lord Randolph, grandson of 7th Duke of Marlborough. Bottom of class at Harrow but passed with high honors from Sandhurst and was commissioned in Fourth Hussars. In all, served in nine British regiments (notably in last British cavalry charge, with 21st Lancers, at Battle of Omdurman, 1898, and in command of battalion of Royal Scots Fusiliers on Western Front, France, 1915–16). War correspondent, Boer War, captured, imprisoned, escaped and capitalized on sudden fame, at age of 25, with lecture tours (of United Kingdom, United States and Canada), thereby setting up a modest fortune which he would supplement with a lifetime of prolific journalism.

Entered parliament in 1900 as a Conservative but soon switched to Free Trade Liberals, and in 1908 campaigned successfully for unemployment allowances, national sickness insurance, a miner's eight-hour day, unsuccessfully for compulsory education till 17 and abolition of House of Lords. Same year, married Clementine Hozier, by whom he had one son and three daughters.

He was in parliament for more than forty years, changing parties three times, to the vexation of most party loyalists. As First Lord of the Admiralty he modernized the navy and, on his own initiative, mobilized it for action six days before the British ultimatum to Germany in August, 1914. For twenty years, he was held responsible for many disasters of policy, wrongly for the Dardanelles fiasco in the First World War, rightly for the General Strike in 1926 and the mischievous urging of "a King's party" during the abdication crisis of Edward VIII.

Throughout the late thirties, he was resented by all parties, mainly for the boring frequency of his warnings about the menace of Nazi rearmament. In May 1940, when after eight months of the "phoney war" Hitler invaded Luxembourg, Holland and Belgium, Chamberlain was discredited and Churchill, surprisingly, became prime minister of a Coalition government as the only politician the Labour Party would serve under. He braced a listless, and still war-weary, Britain to believe it was heroic, and under his leadership, it became so.

In the 1945 election, after the victory in Europe, Churchill, indifferent to peacetime social reforms, was defeated in a Labour landslide. Six years later, in his late seventies, he returned as Conservative prime minister and, increasingly apathetic and senile, resigned in 1955. Ten years later he died, at the age of ninety, and was accorded a dramatic state funeral, for which he had written the meticulous script.

Anyone who reads much biography must come to be struck sooner or later by the volatility of great men's reputations— a capriciousness quite as unpredictable as the ups and downs of Xerox, IBM, or Gulf & Western. Indeed, since publishers, through their absorption into conglomerates, have had to think and act as trading partners in "the book business," the time may not be far off when they will circulate internal memos alerting the staff to the biographical market trends: Rousseau up, Scott Fitzgerald down fifteen points, Virginia Woolf (like oats and wheat) steady.

Only a year or two ago, it seemed, everything that could be usefully written about Winston Churchill had been written and published. His finest hour—if he is to be considered as an object of public acclaim, and hence as a literary growth stock—came soon after the evacuation from Dunkirk, on the day that the French sued for an armistice. In that moment,

Churchill was symbolized for two continents in David Low's cartoon of a British Tommy, valiant on a storm-drenched rock and waving his fist at a flight of Heinkel bombers: "Very well, alone!" Since then, there have been scores of books about Churchill, over forty of them published since the 1960s. Most of them, from Davenport and Murphy's early little rhapsody to Elizabeth Longford's ritual tribute, have been frank celebrations of an immortal. Sharper and more perceptive judgments have come from A. J. P. Taylor and C. P. Snow and from Violet Bonham Carter's affectionate but incisive memoir. The best of them are concerned to isolate— from a compound of successes and blunders, rooted beliefs, set policies, and brilliant guesses—the essential elements of Churchill's character and his leadership. None of them seriously chips away at the monolith. True, in 1970 Brian Gardner assembled a formidable anthology of parliamentary assaults on Churchill's conduct of the war during the disastrous year of 1942.

Meanwhile, as books about Churchill poured from the presses, the definitive assessment of the great man's life was begun, under the supervision of a trust, by his son, Randolph. He had finished two volumes, and brought the story down to 1914, when he died, in 1968. The official life was thereupon taken up by Martin Gilbert, the Oxford historian who was to complete it in nine volumes, along with all the relevant documents. But already, Churchill, dead since 1965, has achieved the sort of marmoreal reputation that is fixed, not subject to revision—bound in morocco and permanently installed on library shelves alongside Izaak Walton's Donne,

Forster's Dickens, Marshall's Washington, and Douglas Southall Freeman's R. E. Lee.

It ought to be enough to deter any intending biographer, but it did not deter William Manchester, who has put out the first of two promised volumes, a 973-page whopper, *The Last Lion—Winston Spencer Churchill: Visions of Glory,* which begins with a survey of the late-Victorian society into which Churchill was born, in 1874, and ends in 1932 with Lady Astor in Moscow assuring Stalin that Churchill is *"finished"*— "Chamberlain is the coming man."

Mr. Manchester begins with an incomparable social survey of Victorian England. It usually suffices to place the young Churchill in the high society into which he was born or to exploit the shameful contrasts between Disraeli's "two nations." But Mr. Manchester has surveyed the whole range of British society without forced pathos or any more irony than the juxtaposed facts invite: the habits, prejudices, economic resources, rituals, games, chronic diseases of Britain's classes and innumerable subclasses, from hymn-singing Methodists to hunting peers; the social pecking order of the Guards regiments; the comparative wages of a landowner, a private soldier, and a coal miner; the contraceptive habits of the aristocracy and the working classes; the social distinctions of dress flaunted along the scale between a bank clerk and a duke. Against this teeming sociological background Mr. Manchester has mounted in the forefront an impressionist picture of the vast influence of the empire when more than half the world's maritime vessels flew the red ensign, when one civil servant was overseer for every two hundred thousand Indians, when one lone Englishman in Borneo had his own flag and national anthem, and when—outside the quarter of the world that was the acknowledged imperial domain—the inspector general of Chinese customs was Irish, the military adviser to the sultan of Morocco was a Scot and "foreign governments were told where to build new lighthouses."

Mr. Manchester then moves on to the boyhood and youth, a dullish period commonly summarized in the boy's devotion to his nanny, the kindly and mountainous Mrs. Everest; his poor marks at Harrow; a cool relation with his father and the wistful contemplation of his mother as "the evening star—I loved her dearly, but at a distance." But Mr. Manchester gives more than a hundred pages, alive with the most engrossing research, to present the record of a boyhood that is pitiable when it is not heartbreaking. The son of an adored and highly neurotic father who disliked him from the start and of a glittering socialite to whom motherhood was a calling as alien as the priesthood, he arrived at Harrow an emotional orphan. He reacted as a spirited boy bereft of affection might be expected to: he demanded attention by becoming a show-off, a practical joker, and the despair of his surrogate parents, the teachers. Deciding to despise the regular syllabus—math, Latin, Greek, and French—he holed up alone to memorize bits of Shakespeare and Macaulay, and soon found himself at the bottom of his class. All the while, he received peppery, scolding letters from his father. He wrote pleading little letters to his mother ("Please write something kind to me"), and she responded, rarely, with the irritability of a fashion model cursed with a squalling brat. In his ten years away at school—whether in health or in dire sickness—he had only one visit from each parent. Even in a period and a country in which upper-class boys were kept under permanent house arrest in the nursery before being exiled to their public school, the brilliant, the beautiful, the appalling Jennie Jerome was the most uncaring of mothers. Apart from her chronic annoyance at her son's well-maintained status as the dumbbell of the school, the only strong emotion she appears to have felt for him was disgust at his having passed on the measles to her favorite lover.

So the education of Winston began in his twenty-second year at an unlikely time and in the most improbable place: the intellectual barren of a fashionable cavalry regiment posted to India—for a nine-year stretch of duty!—in the twilight of the Victorian age. Before his troopship sailed, he heard a friend use the word "ethics." Arrived in Bangalore, he wondered about it: "But here . . . there was no one to tell me about Ethics for love or money." Later, he overheard a man drop the phrase "the Socratic method." He wondered again. He was told that Socrates was an argumentative Greek hounded by a nagging wife into suicide. He had been dead, Churchill discovered, over two thousand years, yet some "method" of his was still being debated. "Such antagonisms," he wrote, "do not spring from petty issues. Evidently Socrates had called something into being long ago which was very explosive. Intellectual dynamite! A moral bomb! But there was nothing about it in *The Queen's Regulations.*" He wrote to his mother and asked her to ship out to him Gibbon's *Decline and Fall,* to be followed by Winwood Reade's *Martyrdom of Man,* a translation of Plato's *Republic,* and twelve volumes of Macaulay. Through the burning Indian days, he devoured these books "till the evening shadows proclaimed the hour" of his other passion, polo. His mother responded with un-characteristic alacrity, for once her son had chosen to be a soldier and was comfortably removed to India, safe from in-trusion on her unflagging round of house parties, balls, love affairs, foreign cruises, and the like, she was able to begin to express some concern for him as an individual rather than as a family pest. And when he made it clear, in insistent letters home, that he meant to make his mark in politics she warmed to an ambition as impatient as her husband's and used her beauty to wheedle, nudge, hector, and even seduce some of the most influential men in England in the cause of her son's lust for preferment.

Much of this has been recounted over and over, not least by Churchill himself, though with such extreme filial respect that he suppresses even a whisper of complaint against his wretched parents. But the story is usually told skimpily and sentimentally, as an object lesson in the doltishness of par-ents and schoolmasters who failed to recognize what we, the latter-day seers, could have told them—that they had on their hands a genius in embryo. Mr. Manchester, however—gratefully admitting that he has been privileged to work "in tandem" with Martin Gilbert—has had at his disposal such an abundance of letters, documents, onlooking comments and opinions that he can afford not to anticipate an event, a quirk of character, or a sign of approaching maturity. His mastery of this huge file of research enables him to introduce us, by way of new and dramatic emphases, to many startling things we thought we knew. It is the same with the rest of Churchill's youthful life abroad: his time as a cavalry subaltern, his dashing off to cover the guerrilla warfare in Cuba, his vaulting over the officer establishment to be present at the Khyber Pass and the Battle of Omdurman, his capture by the Boers and the chronicle of his escape and aimless wandering in search of sanctuary. From Mr. Manchester's account of this five-year safari, we become freshly aware of one of those untrammeled Victorian adventurers, usually highborn but inexplicably inured to discomfort, whose curiosity moves them to treat continents as obvious maps of the Old Boy network and treks into deserts or remote mountain villages as suburban excursions. The young Churchill, who appears to have transformed a frail physique into a tough one by an exercise of free will unknown to physical therapy, was at home in rancid heat and paralyzing cold, on battlefronts, in filthy trains, on a horse or a mule or on foot in the harshest landscapes. (It is a reminder of this vanished type that the most serious accident of his life occurred when he looked the wrong way as he stepped off a New York sidewalk and was knocked down by an automobile.)

This rousing drama, told always with a sure sense of what mattered to Churchill at the time, inevitably slows down and becomes at once more mundane and more debatable when the twenty-six-year-old settles into Parliament. But here, again, in dealing with Churchill's early and middle political career—with material that has been exhaustively mined—

Mr. Manchester makes constant use of the one advantage that all good historians ought to exercise in writing about the life of a nation that is not their own. As an American, he takes nothing for granted, he investigates what the natives assume to be common knowledge, he probes into the origin of institutions as recondite as the parliamentary code of behavior and as ordinary as the bicycle craze, the "pea souper" fog, and WH Smith's newsstands. I doubt whether any English historian would have bothered to describe, for example, the grades of power implicit in the physical layout of the House of Commons, or, having bothered, would have done it in six sentences:

Directly beneath the timbered ceiling lay the well, with the carved chair of the Speaker, who determined which members should have the floor. On either side of the benches, upholstered in green, rose five tiers. Those to the Speaker's right were occupied by the party in power; the Opposition sat to his left. Each tier was separated at midpoint by an aisle, the "gangway." The front government bench, extending from the Speaker's chair to the gangway, was reserved for the prime minister and his cabinet; it was also called "the Treasury Bench" because the first prime minister, Sir Robert Walpole, had also been first lord of the Admiralty and chancellor of the Exchequer. Two red stripes on the well carpet marked the point beyond which no frontbencher would advance in addressing the House; the distance between the stripes was the length of two drawn swords.

These accumulated merits, of scrupulous research, sustained narrative lucidity (he is very fine on the Dardanelles), unabashed inquisitiveness, seem to me to outweigh most of the errors—of judgment, mainly—that Mr. Manchester can be charged with: that he overrates Churchill's political importance in his early parliamentary career; that he has a shaky grasp of Irish politics; that he fails to set against a rapacious, mercantile view of the empire the labors of a generation of able and humane administrators inspired by the example of Lord Lugard, the pioneer colonial administrator of Nigeria, of whom there is no mention. Certainly misgivings about Mr. Manchester's judgment in general creep in when he gives equal credence to, say, the transcript of a parliamentary debate and Frank Harris's ludicrous account of how Lord Randolph picked up syphilis. Harris was a bold and imaginative editor, but his testimony on sexual shenanigans—his own or anyone else's—has long ago been discredited as mischievous fantasy. I suppose a book so packed with new and old documentary material on so many well-rehearsed themes is bound to provoke a fuss of pedants. But on the main theme, on Churchill himself, Mr. Manchester is hospitable to every pro and con, every admiring or malicious comment, every shred of damning or vindicating evidence. As he did in his MacArthur biography, he demonstrates that he is unperturbed by the sharpest and most contrary judgments of his subject. He accepts the largest contradictions in behavior, evidently adopting as an elementary duty of a biographer Shaw's maxim "No specific virtue or vice in a man implies the existence of any other specific virtue or vice in him." The equanimity of this approach is rare, especially in biographies that come to be accepted as classics. One thinks of Sandburg's Lincoln, of Catherine Drinker Bowen's ludicrous life of Justice Holmes, of many of the cameo portraits in Bruce Catton—instances in which the biographer is so tenderly concerned to establish the integrity, if not the canonization, of the subject that sinister rumors are derided, critics are routed, the exposition of the passage from the womb to the tomb becomes a celebration of the guaranteed good life. As a technical matter simply—a flaw in contriving the dramatic movement of a biography—this approach steadily deflates all suspense, because the author is telling you in advance of any provocation how to feel. It is an anxiety rather like that of the directors of movies who hasten to allay a fear (that we are not getting the emotional point) by introducing the persuasion of sobbing violins. From this common but fatally slackening trick Mr. Manchester is almost totally free. He shares the advantage that A. J. P. Taylor has over most scholarly biographers in daring to move, with a fresh, unblinkered eye, into territory that the academics have staked out as their very own, which they contemplate with the unction of long familiarity, and into which they deeply resent the invasion of squatters.

What we have, in the end, is the phenomenon of an impenitent Victorian who, while never ceasing to yearn for the high noon of imperial Britain, had an intuitive feel for the next lurch of history and was able, with the old weapon of his now deeply felt oratory, to goad a sleeping nation to meet it. Many of his convictions, early and late, are now embarrassing to read about: his contemptuous view of Gandhi; his abhorrence of the "unnatural" idea of the women's vote; his love of war and tolerance of it in even its grisliest aspects (the rodents in the trenches of the First World War "played a very useful role in eating human bodies"). But much of this embarrassment is the shame of seeing a man out of his time, like finding a strong vein of hypocrisy in Jefferson's protestations about liberty from the fact of his owning slaves. Along with much Victorian cant, Churchill had, and carried from early manhood into the conduct of the Second World War, Victorian virtues that exhilarated or exasperated his colleagues and overawed his subordinates: a habit of inexhaustible industry; a relentless attention to the details of political and military action; an impatience with small talk; the assumption that twenty-four hours a day are hardly enough for the discovery of the marvels of the world we live in. To these he added some formidable virtues of his own: the acceptance of humiliating defeats as episodes natural to the wielding of power; a tough but generous relationship with political rivals; immediate magnanimity toward a defeated enemy; a willingness to experiment beyond the accepted wisdom of the professional (to invent the tank, to suggest floating landing piers, to declare common citizenship with the French). Above all, in the supreme crisis of national survival, his absolute refusal—unlike many good and prudent men around him—to compromise or surrender.

An old English friend who served in the British embassies both in Washington and Moscow was always "put off by his [Churchill's] brutality, his contempt for the lesser breeds without the law, his lust for war, and so on"; nevertheless, he thought of him as a hero "because I think he saved our lives, and I expect that under my old chief Lord Halifax we should have made peace in 1940 and been successfully invaded after, or before the defeat of Russia."

This heroic period—the spring and summer of 1940—is what everybody now takes for granted and is indeed just about the only thing popular historians and television docudrama directors know about him. It makes his salvation—and ours—all the more marvelous if we recall the prevailing view of him, in the House of Commons and in the country at large, throughout the two decades during which he was looked on as an eccentric and disillusioned political chameleon who had never fulfilled the promise of his youth.

So early as 1921, when Churchill was forty-seven, a London journalist, Harold Begbie, famous for the perceptiveness of his character sketches of politicians, wrote this remarkable passage:

> Happily for himself, and perhaps for the nation, Mr. Churchill lacks the unifying spirit of character which alone can master the antagonistic elements in a single mind. Here is a man of truly brilliant gifts, but you cannot depend upon him. His love for danger runs away with his discretion. I am not enamored of the logic of consistency; on the other hand, who can doubt that one who appears this moment fighting on the left and the next moment on the right creates distrust in both armies. His power is the power of gifts, not character. Men watch him, but they do not follow him.

His faults are chiefly the effects of a forcible and impetuous temperament. They may be expected to diminish with age, but character does not emerge from the ashes of temperament. All Mr. Churchill needs is the direction in his life of a great idea. That is to say that to be saved from himself, he must be carried away by some great ideal, so much greater than his own place in politics that he is willing to face death for its triumph.

At the present Mr. Churchill is in politics as a man is in business, but politics for Churchill, if he is ever to fulfill his promise, must have nothing to do with Churchill. It must have everything to do with the salvation of mankind. . . . [But] it is not to be thought that Mr. Churchill is growing a character which will emerge and create devotion in his countrymen.

This could just as well have been written at any time within a year or two of the outbreak of the Second World War, except that nothing remarkable was any longer expected of him. His career would be said to end with a three-year stretch during which he became something of a nuisance and a bore, a man with a bee in his bonnet about the threat of the Nazi air force. Then came the tenth of May, 1940, when, "at the outset of this mighty battle [the Nazi invasion of the Lowlands and France, the true beginning of the war] I acquired the chief power in the state, which I wielded in ever-growing measure for five years and three months of world war, at the end of which time, all our enemies having surrendered unconditionally or being about to do so, I was immediately dismissed by the British electorate from all further conduct of their affairs."

Despite some dramatic oversimplification and some disturbing eruptions of bloodshot prose, Mr. Manchester's work has such control over a huge and moving narrative, such illumination of character, and such a steady acceptance of the contrariness of a remarkable man seen in the round, that he can claim to have assembled enough powerful evidence in support of Isaiah Berlin's judgment of Churchill as "the largest human being of our time."

23

The Gentleman
from Georgia

(1996)

JONES, ROBERT TYRE JR. Lawyer, engineer, scholar, amateur golfer.
b. March 17, 1902. Son of Robert Tyre Jones, lawyer. For first five years was enfeebled by a puzzling disease. But at age six, won Atlanta East Lake Club's children's championship. At fourteen, was Georgia amateur champion and went through to quarter final of U.S. Amateur championship. In following two years, won Southern amateur. Throughout 1918, the sixteen-year-old toured in exhibition matches on behalf of the Red Cross and War Relief.
ed. public schools of Atlanta till age of fifteen, when he entered Georgia Institute of Technology. Graduated three years later with degree in mechanical engineering. At age eighteen, in 1920, began to enter open golf championships, and continued to play in them for next eight years, during the summer vacations from his studies. 1923, honors degree in English literature, Harvard; won his first U.S. Open championship. After a brief fling at real estate, in 1926 he entered Emory University Law School and after three semesters passed Georgia bar examination. He consequently withdrew and set up law practice, which he maintained for most of his life. He was essentially a weekend golfer, in the fall and the spring.

In 1924 he married Mary Rice Malone, of Atlanta. They had three children.

Between 1923 and 1930, Jones entered twenty major championships, won thirteen and came second in four. During that time, the leading two professionals of the day, Walter Hagen and Gene Sarazen, never won a British or United States Open that Jones entered. In eight years of Walker Cup competition, he won all his singles matches. In the summer of 1930, he won in succession the U.S. Open, the British Open, the British Amateur and the U.S. Amateur, subsequently called "the Grand Slam," a feat never performed before or since. Jones thereupon retired from competitive golf at the age of twenty-eight. In 1930, a group of friends purchased an abandoned southern nursery, which had served as the fruit farm for the Confederate armies. On these 360 acres, Jones, with the help of Scottish architect Dr. Alister Mackenzie, designed the Augusta National golf course. With financier Clifford Roberts, he founded the Augusta National Golf Club and a Jones's invitational tournament, later called (against Jones's wish) the Masters.

In the Second World War, although deferred as a forty-year-old father of three and suffering a medical disability, he was commissioned in Army Air Force intelligence and served in Europe under Eisenhower's command. In 1948, a painful back compelled him to give up golf. After two operations, he was diagnosed with a rare degenerative disease, which progressively paralyzed him. In 1958, he was given the freedom of the city (burgh) of St. Andrews, Scotland. He died in Atlanta, in December 1971.

On the centennial of the birth of Mr. Justice Holmes, I was asked to write a commemorative piece for a liberal weekly. By that time, his reputation as a liberal hero was as secure as Jane Austen's new reputation as a pioneer feminist, an elevation that, if she were within earshot, would—as she might say—"vastly astound" her. Holmes had been so exhaustively written about, so firmly established as the Great Dissenter, that there seemed very little to say about him. I accordingly said very little and summed it all up in the title of the piece: "What Have We Left for Mr. Justice Holmes?" It took many years, and the leisure to look him over freed from his obituary pigeonhole, to make the alarming discovery that the cases in which he voted with the conservative majority as against it were in the ratio of eight or ten to one; and that two notable scholars succeeded each other in spending years preparing his biography only to abandon it to a third man who saw what they had seen in Holmes, but one who also had the courage to say it out loud: that Holmes's political philosophy was (his concern for free speech apart) as fine an intellectual approximation to Fascism as you would care to find among the savants of the Western world.

I have come to a similar hurdle with Robert Tyre Jones Jr. though one nothing like so formidable or alarming. I don't suppose any other athletic hero, certainly no one in golf, has been written about so often and with so much reverence. The same admirable anecdotes are repeated whenever his name is mentioned: his debunking of the teaching clichés ("never up, never in"); his famous putdown by Harry Vardon ("did you ever see a worse shot than that?"); his identifying the enemy as "Old Man Par"; his calling a two-stroke penalty on himself to lose a championship ("you might as well praise a man for not robbing a bank"). And on and on. I have heard these stories a hundred times and concluded long ago that fresh anecdotes about Jones are as few and far between as new funny golf stories. This must be, then, a small memoir of a short friendship in the last years of his life and what I gleaned about him and his character.

In the summer of 1965, when I had been for nearly twenty years the chief American correspondent of the (then *Manchester*) *Guardian,* our golf correspondent, Pat Ward-Thomas, for some reason or other was unable to cover the U.S. Open championship, which was being held, I believe for the first time, at Creve Coeur in St. Louis. I filled in for him and my last day's dispatch eventually appeared in the *Guardian's* annual anthology of the paper's writing. Somehow, a copy of it got to Jones. He wrote me a letter saying, as I recall, he was unaware that "golf was another string to your bow." Why he should have known anything about my "bow" was news to me. But he mentioned that he had been a regular viewer of *Omnibus,* a ninety-minute network television potpourri of drama, science, politics, history, ballet, and God knows what, which I hosted in the 1950s. Jones's letter was, of course, highly flattering to me, especially since this was the first piece I had ever written about golf. I had taken up the game only one year before, at an advanced age (in my mid-fifties— hopeless, I know); but, being a journalist, I started to write about it, just as when you run into a man who is an expert on the manufacture of heels for ladies' shoes—as was a man I met in Rainelle, West Virginia—you write about *him.*

There was another short exchange or two, in one of which Jones characteristically started a letter: "Dear Alistair (don't you think we ought to put an end to this minuet of Mr. Jones and Mr. Cooke?)" and went on to ask me to be sure to call on him whenever I was down in Augusta or Atlanta. Which I did, most often in the company of Ward-Thomas.

My first impression was the shock of seeing the extent of his disability, the fine strong hands, twisted like the branches of a cypress, gamely clutching a tumbler or one of his perpetual cigarettes in a holder. His face was more ravaged than I had expected, from the long-endured pain I imagine, but the embarrassment a stranger might feel about this was tempered by the quizzical eyes and the warmth his presence gave off. (He kept on going to Augusta for the Masters until two years before the end. Mercifully, for everyone but his family, we would not see him when he could no longer bear to be seen.)

After that first meeting I never again felt uncomfortable about his ailment, and only once did he mention it, which was when he spoke a sentence that has passed into the apocrypha. Pat well knew that Jones never talked about his disease, but on that day he really wanted to penetrate the mask of courage and know just how good or bad things really were. Pat's expression was so candid that—I sensed—Jones felt he would, for once, say a word of two. He said that he'd been told that his disease occurred in two forms—"descending and ascending,"* that luckily his paralysis had been from the waist and his extremities down, so that, he added, "I have my heart and lungs and my so-called brain." He spoke about it easily with a rueful smile, and no more was said. The familiar punch line, "You know, we play the ball where it lies," was not said in my presence and, I must say, it sounds to me false to Jones's character, as of a passing thought by a screenwriter that Hollywood would never resist. Let us thank God that Hollywood has never made a movie about Jones; it would almost surely be as inept and more molassic than the dreadful *Follow the Sun,* the alleged "epic" about Ben Hogan.

About the disease. At a tournament Jones was playing in, in England, Henry Longhurst, the late, great rogue of English golf writing, was standing beside a doctor who, mar-

---

* *I have consulted several neurologists about this. None is aware of this distinction but all say that it can begin by attacking different parts of the body in different victims.*

veling at Jones's huge pivot, the long arc of his swing and the consequent muscular strain that sustained it, predicted that one day it would cause him grievous back trouble. Longhurst wrote and retailed this comment to Jones, who responded with a good-tempered note saying, with typical tact, that Henry was good to be concerned but the trouble was due to a rare disease. This sad turn in Jones's life has also received several versions. So far as I can discover, from tapping the memory of his oldest surviving friend, the inimitable Charlie Yates, and checking with the expertise of several medicos, the true account is simple and drastic.

In the summer of 1948, Jones remarked to Yates, in the middle of what was to be his last round ever, that he would not soon be playing again because his back had become un-bearable and he was going to have an operation. It was, in fact, the first of two operations and it revealed damage to the spinal tissue that could not then be tagged with a definite di-agnosis. A year or two later, Jones went up to Boston and af-ter being examined at the Lahey Clinic had the second operation, during which a positive diagnosis was made: sy-ringomyelia, a chronic progressive degenerative disease of the spinal cord, which, as we all know, Jones bore for twenty-two years with chilling stoicism. The scant consolation for the rest of us is that anyone falling victim to the same disease today could expect no better outcome. The etiology is still unknown and there is no cure.

When I first went into the sitting room of Jones's cottage at Augusta, I noticed at once a large picture over the mantel-piece, a framed series of cartoon strips by the best, and throughout the 1920s and 1930s, the most famously popular English sports cartoonist, Tom Webster. No American I knew (and no Englishman under seventy) had ever heard his name, but the drawings—of Jones and of Hagen, I believe—served as a taproot into Jones's memories of Britain and British golf in the 1920s. He enlightened me about the character and skill of various old heroes I brought up: Braid and Duncan and Tolley and Roger Wethered and, of course, Hagen. (Though I played no golf I followed it—from the papers, the newsreels, and the Webster cartoons—as zealously as I followed county cricket). This talk brought up, one time, the never-ending controversy about the essential characteristic of the good golf swing. Jones distrusted "keep your eye on the ball" almost as much as Tommy Armour did. His preference was for Abe Mitchell's "the player should move freely beneath himself."

Jones never recalled to me, as all famous athletes are apt to do, the acclaim of his great days, though once when I had just come back from St. Andrews, he remarked again what a "wonderful experience" it had been on his later visits "to go about a town where people wave at you from doorways and windows." Otherwise, he never said anything that made me doubt his friends' assurance that he was uncomfortable with the spotlight and was grateful to have room service in the hotels of towns where he would be recognized on the streets. He did not flaunt his trophies at home, and he kept his medals locked up in a chest.

Our talks were mostly about books, people, politics, only rarely about golf, whenever Ward-Thomas was eager for another Jones quote for his bulging file of golfing wisdom. In the winter after my first meeting, a book came out entitled *Bobby Jones on Golf,* and I reviewed it under the heading, "The Missing Aristotle Papers on Golf," remarking along the way that Jones's gift for distilling a complex emotion into the barest language would not have shamed John Donne; that his meticulous insistence on the right word to impress the right visual image was worthy of fussy old Flaubert; and that his unique personal gift was "to take apart many of the club clichés with a touch of grim Lippmannesque humor." Shortly after the piece appeared, Jones dropped me a letter beginning: "Off hand, I can't think of another contemporary author who has been compared in one piece to Aristotle, Flaubert, John Donne and Walter Lippmann!"

Much was made—rightly—when the book came out about the extraordinary fact that Jones had written it himself. This is only to remark, in a more interesting way, how phenomenally rare it is for a scholar to become a world-class athlete. The same dependence on a ghost is true of actors and actresses, as also of ninety percent of the world's—at least the Western world's—best politicians. The exceptions are rare indeed. Churchill, after a Washington wartime meeting with Roosevelt, flew home in a bomber, alternating between the controls and the composition of a speech on a pad. He was no sooner in London than he appeared at the BBC and broadcast across the Atlantic a majestic strategical survey of the world at war. To his horror, Roosevelt heard it in the White House while he was working on his own promised broadcast with the aid of three ghost writers. One of them,

Robert Sherwood, consoled the president with the sorrowful thought: "I'm afraid, Mr. President, he rolls his own."

When I think back to those Augusta talks, I recall most vividly the quality of irony that was always there in his eyes and often in his comments on people and things. I asked him once about "the master eye" without knowing that he had written about it. I'm sure he said what he had said before: he didn't believe in it or in the ritual of plumb bobbing. The main thing was to "locate the ball's position . . . I'm told a man can do this better with two eyes than with one." The last time I saw him, I told him about a rather morose Scottish caddie I'd recently had who took a dim view of most things American, but especially the golf courses, which—he'd been told—had lots of trees. We were sitting out on the porch of his Augusta cottage and Jones looked down at the towering Georgia pines, the great cathedral nave, of the plunging tenth fairway. "I don't see," he said deadpan, "any need for a tree on a golf course."

Toward the end of one Masters tournament, Henry Longhurst took suddenly very ill. He lay grumpily in his hospital bed and, lifting his ripe W. C. Fields's nose over the bedsheet, predicted that it was "closing time." Happily, it turned out not to be, but Pat and I stayed over through the Monday to watch out for him. In the early afternoon, when the place was empty, we called on Jones and he suggested we collect some clubs from the pro shop and play the splendid par three course. We were about to set off when Cliff Roberts, co-founder of the club, came in. He was shocked at the generosity of Jones's suggestion: "Bob, you surely know the

rule—no one can play without a member going along."
"Don't you think," Jones asked wistfully, "you and I could exercise a little Papal indulgence?" Roberts did not think so.
And although he'd recently had a major operation, he went
off, got into his golfing togs and limped around with us
through six holes, by which time he was ready for intensive
care and staggered away accepting the horrid fact of the broken rule.

Because of the firm convention of writing nothing about
Jones that is less than idolatrous, I have done a little digging
among friends and old golfing acquaintances who knew him
and among old and new writers who, in other fields, have a
sharp nose for the disreputable. But I do believe that a whole
team of investigative reporters, working in shifts like coal
miners, would find that in all of Jones's life anyone had been
able to observe, he nothing common did or mean.

However, a recent author, in a book depicting the Augusta
National club as a CEO's Shangri-la, does not spare the patron saint of golf from his lamentations. He attacks Jones on
two counts. First, for his being "weak and irresolute" in bowing to Cliff Roberts's expulsion of a player for violating the
etiquette of the game. (On the contrary, Jones was disturbed
by the man's behavior for six years. Only when, after three requests, the man properly apologized, did Jones welcome him
back.) This criticism reflects a serious misconception about
Jones's function. In the running of the Masters, Cliff
Roberts's power was absolute. What Jones brought to the
tournament was the prestige of his immense popularity, not
to mention a saving contribution of seed money when the

club was on the verge of foundering. Otherwise, it was understood from the start that Roberts was the prime mover and shaker, the organizer of the staff and the commissary, the recruiter and commander of the course patrols, the boss of the course officials and of crowd control, the inventor of new conventions of scoring, and even (over Jones's protesting pleas) the final judge of the architecture of a hole.

So the view of Jones as the impotent puppet king of a cabal of CEOs is both melodramatic and quite wrong. In the beginning, Jones and Roberts wrote to hundreds of friends, acquaintances and strangers "to buy a share of the club" but recruited only a minuscule membership: a hundred dollars a head was hard to come by in the pit of the Depression. Incidentally, the slur also blandly ignores the deepening agony of Jones's illness throughout the last twenty years of his attendance at "his" tournament. (His private view of the tycoon's preserve that Augusta was to become was never, I believe, vouchsafed to his friends, but it was after a hearty get-together of board chairmen, celebrated in a photo opportunity more theirs than his, that he confided ruefully: "They say I love people. I don't. I love a few people in small doses.")

The second charge is more familiar and these days has become inevitable when a young author reacts to warm praise of an old southerner. It is the charge of "racism." This is so pretentiously silly that I have to swallow hard to choose to meet it. It is the old fallacy, which every generation is subject to, of judging a man outside his time and place. Franklin Roosevelt now, I imagine, is thought in retrospect to have had a very callous streak since he never protested the separation of the races. Many shocked readers of this piece would have felt the same indifference if they had been born a half century earlier. I know. I was there. During my first two years in America, I was curious about, but not outraged by, the social status of the Negroes. In my most enlightened moments I should have thought of them as an aberration in an otherwise admirable system. The Negro was not yet a crusade, even among bloodshot liberals.

I look back on the southerners I knew and admired. I was lucky to have traveled far and wide in the South in the 1930s and 1940s, and I had many friends in many southern places. Jones belonged to those fine ones who were incapable of condescending to a black or being ever less than conscious of their lowly status. When things went wrong for their servants—sickness, debt, delinquency—the family took anxious care of them, of its own. By contrast, we in the North hired daily help in good conscience and hoped they stayed well. Their private afflictions were their own. The northern Negro might be permitted more public chutzpah than his southern brother, but the North took it out in tuberculosis.

For myself, I can now say simply that in my life I can count four human beings who radiated simple goodness: my father; a Franciscan priest; a university professor; and Robert Tyre Jones Jr. Maybe "radiated" is too strong a word, for one striking thing about good human beings is their gift for not being striking. Jones had an instinct for noticing, and attending to, the shy one in any bubbling company. His capacity for shifting the spotlight away from himself was remarkable even in the one performance where you would expect him to be authoritative: in the act of teaching golf. In those precious film shorts he made for the Warner brothers, in which a lesson in the use of the brassie or mashie is tagged on to a ludicrous plot about a golf widow or other domestic strain, he never says "you must do this . . ." or "it is essential to do that." He is careful always to say: "I've found that if I move the ball an inch or so . . ." and "perhaps if you tried . . . it works well with some people."

The last indelible memory of him, for those who had the luck to be in St. Andrews in the late autumn of 1958, was his acceptance of the freedom of the city. The Provost was careful to say that he was being saluted not only as "the first golfer of this age . . . but as a man of courage and character." In response, Jones put aside the notes he had painfully written out and spoke freely, first of the Old Course, which had enraged the nineteen-year-old and come to enchant the man; then he talked with the slightest tremor of the curious lasting friendship he had acquired for a city and a people "who have a sensitivity and an ability to extend cordiality in ingenious ways."

He hobbled off to his electric golf cart and began to propel it down the center aisle, as the audience stirred, picked up the cue of a tentative voice, and rose to sing "Will Ye No' Come Back Again?" The start of the hobble and the fact of the cart were enough to remind them that he never would. It was a moment of suddenly shared emotion that upset the most cynical. Herbert Warren Wind remarked: "It was ten minutes before many who attended were able to speak with a tranquil voice." During those minutes, he seemed to one on-looker to qualify for Frederick Buechner's definition of goodness as "valor and unnatural virtue."

What we are left with in the end is a forever young, good-looking southerner, an impeccably courteous and decent man with a private ironical view of life who, to the great good fortune of people who saw him, happened to play the great game with more magic and more grace than anyone before or since.